BIG
CAREER IN THE
BIGCITY

LAND A JOB AND GET A LIFE IN NEW YORK

BY VICKI SALEMI

JIST Works
America's Career Publisher

Big Career in the Big City

© 2010 by Vicki Salemi

Published by JIST Works, an imprint of JIST Publishing
7321 Shadeland Station, Suite 200
Indianapolis, IN 46256-3923
Phone: 800-648-JIST   Fax: 877-454-7839   E-mail: info@jist.com

Visit our Web site at **www.jist.com** for information on JIST, tables of contents, sample pages, and ordering instructions for our many products!

Quantity discounts are available for JIST books. Please call our Sales Department at 800-648-5478 for a free catalog and more information.

Trade Product Manager: Lori Cates Hand
Interior Designer and Page Layout: Toi Davis
Cover Concept: Amy Adams
Cover Design and Layout: Aleata Halbig
Proofreaders: Paula Lowell, Jeanne Clark
Indexer: Kelly D. Henthorne
Printed in the United States of America
15 14 13 12 11 10   9 8 7 6 5 4 3 2 1

Library of Congress Cataloging-in-Publication Data

Salemi, Vicki.
  Big career in the big city : land a job and get a life in New York / Vicki Salemi.
     p. cm.
  Includes index.
  ISBN 978-1-59357-776-6 (alk. paper)
1. Job hunting--New York State--New York. 2. Entry-level employment--New York State--New York. 3. New York (N.Y.)--Guidebooks. I. Title.
  HF5382.75.U62N573 2010
  650.1409747'1--dc22

                              2009052187

ISBN 978-1-59357-776-6

CONTENTS

FOREWORD

I could have used a lot of Vicki Salemi's career advice back in the late '80s when I landed in Manhattan from Miami Beach and was living alone in a small studio above a not-so-nice-smelling restaurant, trying to make a go of it in the Big Apple. Frank Sinatra's words ring oh-so-true to anyone who has ever faced a similar fate in this tough town: *If I can make it there, I'll make it anywhere.*

Vicki shows you how to do just that in this upbeat, cheerful book, but she does not mince words. Her down-to-earth directives start in the early pages with this warning: "If you want to roll up your sleeves and dig into the best city in the world, you gotta face the facts: Not everyone is cut out to live here...You must, must, *must* want it badly. You have to be thirsty for it, be hungry for it, and be open to every opportunity that's out there."

Amen! And as such, *Big Career in the Big City* is more than a job search guide. It's about establishing a career *and* a life, with plenty of great advice, from getting a New York area code for your contact number so recruiters won't think they have to pay to relocate you from Peoria, to other little gems. Among my favorites: "Expect the best for yourself, but remember you won't always start at the top."

Her book is particularly relevant to young women right now because of the challenging job market as well as the ever-present fascination that the city holds for so many twenty-somethings.

Big Career will make you more powerful, more independent, and more confident as you launch a life and career that most people only dream of achieving. Vicki is uniquely qualified to deliver this advice because not only did she make the move from the suburbs to the fabulous big-city life, but she also worked as a recruiter for a global powerhouse, so she knows the ins and outs of the job hunting business.

Last but not least, all this information is delivered in a lively and friendly style that sets it apart from many of the more straightforward offerings on the market. Every girl can use a little sizzle to her style—and Vicki offers up plenty of that.

So start spreading the news. Enjoy your job search in the city that never sleeps. This is Vicki Salemi's New York, New York.

Tory Johnson
CEO, Women For Hire; author, *Fired to Hired: Bouncing Back from Job Loss to Get to Work Right Now*

ACKNOWLEDGMENTS

I would like to express sincere gratitude to my wonderful editor, Lori Cates Hand, and the fabulous team at JIST, including their terrific publicist, Selena Dehne. Thank you for making this book a reality! It's super exciting to be part of this creative team.

Special thanks to my support system, including Jennifer Macaluso-Gilmore's guiding force and her inspirational Divas; my mentors Gina LaGuardia, founder of Gina LaGuardia Editorial Services, and Tory Johnson, the empowering CEO of *Women for Hire*; fellow alumni from my awesome alma mater, Lafayette College; all of the fabulous sources who took time out of their busy schedules to be interviewed for this book; and last but not least, my family.

Above all, this book wouldn't exist if it wasn't for my exhilarating partner in crime: New York City. Mwuah!

To my wonderful parents, Maxine and Gerald R. Salemi.
I love you very much.

ARE YOU READY FOR THE BIG TIME?

Pssst. Over here. Yeah you, I'm talkin' to you. Can you hear me? Come closer, closer, there…just about right.

I heard through the grapevine that you want a scintillating job and sexy little life right in the heart of New York City. True? Alrighty, then. I'm your fairy career godmother. (Ooh—not liking the sound of that. Godmother sounds so very old and way too Cinderella-ish.) How 'bout this instead: I'm your career goddess. Your Gotham goddess. Your career goddess in Gotham! There, much better.

I'm here to give you some tough love (more Simon Cowell than Paula Abdul from *American Idol*—that is, when Paula was on *Idol*) with a whole lot of sass and in-your-face advice! After all, if you want to roll up your sleeves and dig into the best city in the world, you gotta face the facts: Not everyone is cut out to live here.

So, that said, are you sure this is for you? Now, I know the little voice in your head is thinking in all italics: "*Why would this author write an awesome comprehensive big career AND big city guide if she didn't want me to buy it?*" Because I'm an honest career goddess, that's why.

Granted, you're going to need to get a job no matter what, but you'll need a special big-kahuna skill set to land one when you're not already in the know (and by that, I mean not already living in the big city). But, not everyone is cut out for Manhattan. If you want to move to the Big Apple because you've seen it in the movies and can't wait to dish with the gals over martinis and Manolos a la *Sex and the City*, move on. If you think it's plucked right out of an episode of the Upper East Side's *Gossip Girl,* it's time to mosey on. This is not the city for you.

I just don't want you to have false expectations, that's all. If you do, however, dream as big as the skyscrapers that kiss the stratosphere and can't wait to make your mark in the city, it's time for you to get on the groove train, 'cuz we're in for a fantabulous ride.

And don't say I didn't warn you: It will indeed be bumpy. Sure, you will get doors slammed in your face and realize that all that glitters is not gold. You'll deal with gossipy or (dare I say) backstabbing co-workers, cutthroat bosses, and rude landlords. You'll handle a roommate or two (or more!) and a mouse or two (let's hope it's not more!). However, you will get a whole lot of *carpe diem* in return and the ability to live a juicy life in all its glory. That's the reason you're packing your bags in the first place, right?

You, too, can wake up in a city that never sleeps to find that you're king of the hill, top of the heap. But here's the deal: You're not the only one looking to make the leap, and you're *so* not the only person who feels entitled to make their mark on a ridiculously juicy city with endless career and social options. Countless other grads and not-so-new alums want a ticket to this exhilarating ride, too. Your shiny diploma and a token (ahem, a little yellow MetroCard) will get you on a subway. For reals.

You gotta think outside the box, leap outside the confines of a gray little cubicle, and get ready to rumble. Ready to rock that career kasbah, roll up your sleeves, and dig into a thrilling job expedition? (Sidebar: was gonna say *journey* but that sounds way too counselor-like, don'tcha think?) Whatcha waiting for?

Here's the deal: You can and totally will hitch a ride on a career comet, but you'll have to think sharper and sparkle brighter than ever in order to stand out, brainiac. Up for the challenge? Goooood. I knew you had it in you.

Your mission, should you choose to accept it, is this: Get ready to work and create your own destiny. As I equip you with all the tools and rules you'll need for the career search, we'll move onto the get-a-life gig. After all, getting a life in a huge city is complicated. There are countless opportunities and endless ways to meet cool people. There will be people who suck your energy and drain you, and waste your time. Others will be a blast and they'll have friends to introduce you to and so on and so on. I'm so psyched for you!

Buyer beware, though: The process itself may feel like it's taking forever. That's because it is. Nah, it won't really take that long, but since you wish your new life would begin tomorrow, anything beyond tomorrow is going to feel long. Do us both a favor and don't put a timeframe around your search. Snagging a job is one thing, but snatching the right one in New York City is quite another. As you escape the notion of time, you'll be set to make your mark.

Manhattan is truly the center of the universe. It's my mojo, my moxie. And soon it will be yours, too. Let's get this party started!

What's Your NYC-ability?

That's right. I'm talkin' your Manhattan mojo and moxie. The fire in your belly that simply says it's NYC or bust, baby! Are you truly ready to become a Gotham gal? Or are you a shrinking violet and more comfortable in the country than the big city? It's pop quiz time, diva!

The thought of getting on a crowded subway during rush hour where it's literally flesh on flesh with odors of pickle breath or random briefcases shoved into your back is

a. Part of the New York experience! What an invigorating way to start the day. For real.

b. Less than ideal, but hey: If it's the fastest way to get to work, I'll have to deal.

c. Gross. I'll walk or take the bus instead, thank you very much.

Paying $1,500 in rent, $15 each day for lunch, $4.50 in subway fares, not to mention other expenses is

a. Worth it. You get what you pay for and NYC is worth every penny.

b. A travesty, but hey: Even though I'll be broke, at least I'll be happy.

c. Absurd.

(CONTINUED)

(CONTINUED)

The idea of paying a ton of money to live in a tiny apartment with two roommates, a makeshift wall, and the occasional mouse is

a. Your typical no-frills housing situation. Bring it!
b. Ick, but still worth it in order to have my shiny new life.
c. Gross and unacceptable.

This Thursday night you can either jet downtown to a cocktail party at a gallery opening, gallivant uptown to a private industry event at a museum, go to happy hour in the Meatpacking District, catch a celebrity book signing at Barnes & Noble on Fifth Avenue, or chill at home. You want to

a. Do it all! But alas, that's not possible. So you'll pick two events that are closest to each other, like the book signing and museum soiree, courtesy of a quick trip on the 6 train.
b. Take a deep breath and then focus on one event, like the cool gallery cocktail party. Ooh la la!
c. Chillax. Home sweet home all the way.

As you're crossing the street and a messenger on a bicycle speeds past a red light, almost literally knocking you down to the pavement, you...

a. Curse him out at the top of your lungs.
b. Shake your head in disbelief and chalk it up to another day as a pedestrian.
c. Curse the dude in the loudest voice possible in your head, curse the city, and make your exit as soon as possible.

Answers:

Mostly *A*s: Congratulations! A magnificent Manhattan life awaits and you're clearly more than ready to bite into the Big Apple. The question though: Is it ready for you?

Mostly *B*s: You're almost there. It may take time to feel completely ready to take on the land of the bright lights coupled with roaches, ridiculous rent prices, and a maxed-out social life. Be patient and realize that perhaps you should take baby steps by living in one of the boroughs.

Mostly *C*s: New York City? Fughettabout it. Hate to break it to you, sweetheart, but since you didn't exactly pass the test, there's no need to push it. If you force it, you'll be unhappy and homesick. New Yawk isn't going anywhere and will be here when you're ready for its magic.

CHAPTER 1

ROCK THE CAREER KASBAH

Congrats! You passed the test in the Introduction with flying colors. After all, some people have goals and don't act on them. You, my friend, are pursuing them full throttle.

You realize the journey to New York may not be easy. Heck, it could get tough at times, and take longer than you anticipated. You're committed, though, so I have no reason to doubt that you'll get what you want and then some.

That said, you'll need to start at the very beginning. Whether you're conducting your job search across the miles or just from someplace else in the eastern time zone, you need to first set the stage for your job search adventure.

How I Fell in Love with New York

First things first: We'll start with me. Since I'll be navigating the search and helping you let your inner New Yorker shine, you might as well hear my story. I totally get where you're coming from. I truly do. That's because several years ago I, too, yearned for something bigger, brighter, and much more spectacular than the suburbs could have ever offered! Yes, my friend, it's true. Yours truly lived in New Jersey.

Isolated and ridiculously bored out of my mind on all fronts (the job, the social life or lack thereof, everything), I slowly started checking my way into Manhattan, which was bizarre because the city had actually always scared me when I was growing up so close to it geographically. The fact that I can't imagine living anywhere else right now is quite ironic. I digress...

Little by little I started going to Manhattan after work or on weekends for various press events and alumni outings. Quickly it became my life-line. I began meeting cool people, expanding my circle, and in turn, felt like I was exposed to a whole new world. I was starting to get a life; and boy, did it feel refreshing. As I was slowly getting the hang of the grid, it started growing on me like a rash (but a good one).

For instance, several years ago for a freelance writing gig my magazine editor sent me to Gotham for a celebrity interview. And I'm not just talkin' any celebrity: how about Angelina Jolie?! (To say I was nervous would be an understatement! I also interviewed other actors in the film and the producer and director.) That exciting day I participated in my very first press day for the film *Lara Croft Tomb Raider: The Cradle of Life,* and my quote endorsing the movie was published in the *New York Times*! During that awesome experience I realized that this city is an amazing place where incredible opportunities unfold. There was no turning back; I was hooked!

I had officially gotten the itch for Manhattan! As I started construct-ing my game plan to get into Gotham, I was sent on a business trip to London for a month while working in my day job, international human resources. That trip solidified my goals: Saying buh-bye to the 'burbs and signing up for sassy city girl life! I planned to make my magnificent move upon returning home. Within a few months of my job search I transferred internally into recruiting while rocking out to journalism, my passion, at night and on weekends. I can honestly say my life became tremendous, spectacular, and downright scintillating. The thrilling ride just keeps getting more exciting and I haven't looked back since! I took ownership and made things happen and that's why I'm super-psyched for you, too!

Several years later, this Manhattanite has certainly found her hap-pily ever after. Between my super-fun jobs (yes, as in plural), amazing friends, cool organizations, and countless cultural activities and press events, there is no place I would rather live, work, and play. I thrive on the excitement, the energy, the *joie de vivre*! For instance, a few weeks ago I was a seatfiller at an awards show and sat in the second row as for-mer President Bill Clinton took the podium. Bill Clinton! Plus, this city lends itself well to specific industries and it's the pulse of my careers.

Initially I worked full-time at the day job in a corporate recruiting role. At night I moonlighted as a journalist and gallivanted around town as a fashionista/entertainment reporter and health/wellness journalist. Recently my role has catapulted me into launching my own business as an executive recruiting and career consulting firm. I love leveraging my corporate background in recruiting and human resources by helping people get awesome new jobs, ramping up their resumes, honing their interviewing skills, the works. I also do public speaking about careers, which has been a blast! In NYC there are limitless ways to make your mark and pursue opportunities that get you juiced.

I still love love love being in writer mode as a freelance journalist with various newspapers, magazines, and Web sites. I primarily tackle topics about careers, health, style, and entertainment, and I most definitely still enjoy conducting those fun celebrity interviews (whenever I have one scheduled I wake up that morning feeling like it's my birthday). They're just as exciting as the first one with Angelina (and definitely not nerve-wrecking at this point). Love it! The 9 a.m. to 6 p.m. day job became a thing of the past as I currently work 24/7 (but it's so much fun and does not feel like work). I now create delicious new projects and live the dream each and every day in the city where amazing things happen. Yeah! Soon I'll be auditioning for television commercials—why not, right? Before I moved I knew that my scrumptious New York City life beckoned my arrival, but I had no idea how delicious it would truly be and how it would consistently evolve and still feel fresh year after year.

As for how I mastered the move? I wanted it badly. You must, must, *must* want it badly. You have to be thirsty for it, be hungry for it, and be open to every opportunity that's out there. Assuming you're in the same place and have established your burning desire for Manhattan despite its tiny quarters, stressful conditions, and yes the occasional unwanted mouse, we need to first dish about the job part.

If you don't have a job, you certainly won't have a life. That is, you won't be able to afford one. I need to pause right now and remind you that a fantastic life is waiting for you. And although it's an expensive life, it's not a glam one all the time. You may live in a tiny apartment with sirens blasting all the time; and if that's for you, keep reading. If it's not, then move to the 'burbs. Anyway, living in Manhattan can get intense and the key is not letting your social life interfere with your day job. The converse is true, too: Not letting your work interfere with your life (half-kidding). The balancing act is critical to surviving and thriving without being sleep deprived. If they're both suffering, it's game over. And if they're both sizzling, as in, "Hey, look at me, I'm on top of the world," that could be problematic as well. You and I both know that when you're sitting pretty, the only way to go is down if you don't have the stamina to keep it going.

Anyway, now that introductions are out of the way, we'll tackle the job stuff first. I actually live for this stuff and get excited dishing about resumes, interviewing, networking, job hunting, and helping people land a juicy job! Next, we'll move onto the getting a life part, which is quite exhilarating.

You game? Ready. Set. Let's go to Gotham already!

Get Ready to Rock

Okay, how many on-campus career advisors or professors have told you that the job search is a big scrumptious par-tay? None, right? I'm here to tell you that it is a celebration—that is, if you allow yourself to embrace the process. Getting a job could be a cool project and one that doesn't simply start and end. Yes, that's right: The job search is a never-ending stream of networking your entire career. So if you don't like it right now, you will eventually, so you might as well learn to like the process sooner rather than later. So that you don't get overwhelmed, though, we'll focus on one job you have to get. Just one. That's it. One.

As we create your job search strategies, let's not lose the vision of what's driving you during the process: Fab job, fantastic life. You've caught the bug and you just can't shake it (nor should you try). Nor should you sit back and wait and expect a job to come knocking on your door. You cannot expect someone to hand you a pretty little job on a platter. If you want something badly enough, you simply have to go after it. Got it?

But the question is, now that you know Manhattan is your game, what's your career name? What are you going after? Do you have a specific industry in mind? Is it financial services? Hospitality? Tourism? Fashion? Media? Health care? Let's start with none. In a way, this is a blessing and also a curse. If you don't know what you want, you have a completely open mind, which keeps you open to countless opportunities. On the other hand, let's face the facts: Not knowing what you want means you'll be here, there, and everywhere without a specific focus.

Resume Writing 101

As you start from scratch, the very first thing you need to do is create your resume. After all, how can you market your skills and abilities if you don't have anything to show for it? Your resume is your calling card, your identity, your secret sauce, if you will. It will set you apart from all the other candidates vying for the same job you're pursuing. Plus, it's your very first foray into showing a company your professionalism and assets.

Okay, you probably already know precisely what a resume is (also known as a CV). But it doesn't hurt to go over the basics.

It's All About Looks

First of all, ensure that it's just one page. When you're right out of school or even in your mid- to late twenties, your CV should not be longer than one page. As for situations when it approaches two (dare I even say three?) pages, well, that occurs when you have years upon years of experience and have published papers or conducted research and become a distinguished professional in your field.

Among other basics? Your resume should be grammar-error-free and not have any typos. You would be shocked at how many people submit resumes with tiny errors, which are a sure-fire way to let your future employer know you're not detail-oriented. Review your resume several times. And if you need a friend to eyeball it as well, by all means do it.

As for the structure of the resume, I prefer crisp and clean without too many font sizes and boldfacing, italics, and underlines. You should want your background to leap off the page, not the 18-point type. The specific font is up to you, without going overly spiffy like script or italics (again, think crisp and clean); but you can't go wrong with Times New Roman.

Putting It Together

Your contact information should be at the top of your resume. Whether it's in the center or left or right justified, it matters not. What does matter is having your name, address, phone number, and e-mail address clearly visible.

> **Note:** *When you're in college you can definitely list your campus address as well as your address back at home. After you graduate, just remember to remove your college address from your resume.*

The objective goes below your contact info. As for whether or not to include an objective at all, the jury's still out on this one. Some hiring managers like it because it shows them specifically what you're seeking and indicates that you're goal-oriented. The other school of thought is that it's not necessary and wastes valuable space. A cover letter should demonstrate your interest in the specific job, thereby making the objective appear redundant.

Some people decide to keep the objective and merely change it based on the job they're pursuing. So in the end, they may have three or four resumes that vary by the objective. I've never seen someone get hired because of an objective, nor have I seen a candidate get rejected because they included one. It's all up to you, so let's not sweat the small stuff.

The good news about pursuing entry-level and early-career positions is just that your resume speaks to your education. Your education should be toward the top of your resume. As you gain more years of work experience, the education piece will slide to the bottom of the resume; but for our purposes, it's toward the top. If your G.P.A. was impressive, by all means mention it! It's not necessary to include it, though, but if it was high you might as well showcase it. If your grade-point average was oh, let's say at 2.8 on a 4.0 scale, better off leaving it on the cutting-room floor.

Other notable items to include are study-abroad programs, honor societies or memberships, and any campus activities. Granted, you don't necessarily need to say that you won an award for most photogenic in your sorority two consecutive years, but if you were the organization's treasurer and you're aiming for a job in accounting, including this extra-curricular activity on your CV/resume will serve you well.

Underneath your education you should list your work experience in reverse-chronological order, starting with the most recent at the top. Now, I know what you're thinking. Whether you're in college or are a brand-spankin'-new graduate, you may not have a lot to include. Think again, my friend. How about any internships you had during the summer or various semesters? What about any special programs you participated in, such as shadowing an alumnus for a few days in their workplace? Or how about a special research project you assisted a professor with? Surely you'll be able to come up with a few important experiences to highlight.

The next skill is important so listen up: Incorporate action verbs so that you literally leap off the page. Don't embellish or lie; instead, simply use captivating words that grab the reader and imply that your work was important. For instance, instead of saying

Filed ongoing paperwork as necessary.

perhaps you can say

Managed daily paperwork and created electronic filing system.

Again, it's important to be truthful and avoid stretching the truth, but sometimes we overlook our accomplishments. Perhaps you trained two high school interns who assisted you with your workload? Most defi-nitely articulate this on your resume:

Conducted training for two high school interns and delegated daily assignments.

Now is the time to shine! If you truly scanned documents and saved them on a hard drive, or if you trained your colleagues, by all means say it.

Toward the bottom of the resume you can indicate your technical skills if they're special. It's a safe assumption that everyone in our generation knows a thing or two about Microsoft Word and Excel. Again, if you put it on your resume it probably won't work against you, but it's not going to distinguish you among other Microsoft whizzes either.

Sample Resumes

Here are a couple of sample resumes for new graduates.

Jen Applicant
123 Main Street
New York, NY 12345
917.123.4567
jen@address.com

OBJECTIVE

To gain employment in human resources utilizing my organizational and interpersonal skills.

EDUCATION

The State University of New York, School of Arts and Sciences—Plattsburgh, NY, *May 2010*

- B.A. in English; GPA in Major: 3.79/4.0; Overall GPA: 3.35/4.0
- Dean's List: 2010
- Study Abroad (Paris, France): Fall 2009

EXPERIENCE

MTV—New York, NY, *Summer 2010*
Human Resources Department, Summer Intern

- Analyzed hiring data and metrics and assisted in conducting new-hire orientations.
- Created electronic filing system.
- Trained new team members.
- Managed internal client relationships.

IBM—Chicago, IL, *Summer 2009*
Human Resources Department, Summer Intern

- Processed new-hire paperwork, including onboarding database.
- Reviewed payroll data for 1,000 employees; liaised with internal payroll department.
- Participated in monthly meetings with internal clients as it pertained to salary review.
- Collected and analyzed annual performance reviews; made suggestions for improvement.

College Newspaper, *2007–2010*
Sports Reporter

- Wrote articles for three collegiate sports teams on a weekly basis.
- Attended weekly games and interviewed players and coaches.
- Submitted copy on tight deadlines.
- Blogged about games from the sidelines.

The School Fund—Plattsburgh, NY, *Summer 2007*
Phone-a-thon Participant

- Called alumni in fund-raising effort to seek donations.
- Lead caller in two categories of reluctant alumni donors.
- Raised $3,000 within ten hours of participation.

ADDITIONAL INFORMATION

Computer: Proficient in Microsoft Office
Freelance Sports Columnist: Featured on sites such as City Paper, Local Magazine
Human Resources Skills: Confidentiality, Multi-tasking, Organizational and Interpersonal Skills

---

Jane Doe
Jane.Doe@emailaddress.com
212.123.4567

Temporary Address: *Permanent Address:*
P.O. Box 1234   123 Maiden Lane
University Park, PA 16802   Lancaster, PA 17602

Education

Pennsylvania State University, University Park, PA
May 2010

- Bachelor of Arts, Business Administration
- Dean's List
- Awarded fellowship in Web database design and network administration.
- Created and presented marketing plan for annual campus-wide entrepreneurial contest; won second place.

Experience

The Crayola Factory
Easton, PA
Brand Marketing Intern
Summer 2009

- Created models for topline growth forecasts for crayons and markers.
- Analyzed public data on products and prepared summaries for management on a weekly basis.
- Developed data analysis tools for Web site to drive brand strategy.
- Coordinated company's distribution strategy with its brand strategy; implemented company-wide.

M&M Mars
Hackettstown, NJ
Marketing Intern
Summer 2008

- Evaluated and reengineered inventory management system.
- Developed marketing campaign for blue M&Ms.
- Created and implemented marketing strategy for peanut M&Ms.
- Analyzed marketing and financial data to spot trends.

Nike v. Reebok Marketing Research Report, Pennsylvania State University
Professor Smith, Marketing Department
Spring 2007

- Conducted campus surveys and extrapolated data as it related to Nike and Reebok shoes.
- Analyzed data and provided results to professor.
- Designed and implemented new marketing plans and suggested them to professor.
- Earned acknowledgments during annual presentation to faculty.

Skills

Proficient in Win 7, Mac OS, MS Office, VBA, HTML, Dreamweaver, CorelDraw, Photo-Paint, Photoshop, Illustrator, Adobe Premiere, FileMaker Pro, Claris Home Page, Xara 3D, Webster, AutoCAD, and C programming language.

References

And oh yeah, you might add a line at the bottom about "References Upon Request." Perhaps I'm a stickler, but I don't think it's necessary. If a hiring manager or recruiter needs references from you, they'll simply ask you. Deleting that line gives you precious space for more important things.

This brings up the next question: Who should be your references? This is yet another reason why resume writing gets me excited! Your references should be people you stay in touch with (ahem, keep the networking swirl going, girl!). Your references should also be people who can talk about your attributes and praise your abilities. Whether it's a professor on campus, an advisor during your internship, or perhaps editor-in-chief of the school newspaper while you were a reporter meeting strict weekly deadlines, reach out to them and ask them if they can vouch for you. This way, when your prospective employer is ready to contact your references, you'll already have their green-light approval, along with their contact info.

Note: *By the way, prior to an interview, you'll need to complete an employment application, which will ask for your contact information, work and education history, the works. Essentially it should mirror your resume such that most companies need an application and resume to process your candidacy in plain ol' paperwork terms. Some applications ask for your references' contact information, so you can always include their deets on the application itself.*

As for whether companies actually call to check references, well, that totally depends on the company. Sometimes companies may certainly call the human resources departments of former employers to verify that information on your resume and application are valid (remember when you felt like fudging dates at your old internship or altering your title? So not a good idea). Others may call to verify both your employment and testimonials. Please don't let this part stress you out; it's part of the employment process. As long as you're truthful on the resume and application and have former bosses, mentors, and advisors to vouch for you, you're good to go.

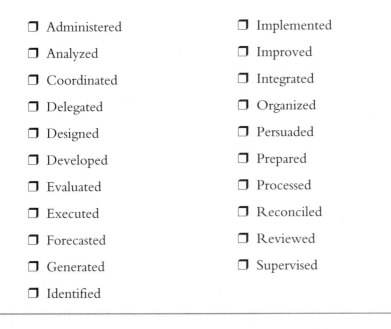

Action Verbs Are Your Friends

Action verbs are powerful and pack a punch. Feel free to vary the verbs so that your resume doesn't look redundant. Assuming the work experience is in the past, your verbs should reflect the past tense as well. Your current position (even if you're currently interning while pursuing a full-time gig) should always allude to verbs in the present tense. Here are some powerful verbs you can use:

❒ Administered   ❒ Implemented

❒ Analyzed   ❒ Improved

❒ Coordinated   ❒ Integrated

❒ Delegated   ❒ Organized

❒ Designed   ❒ Persuaded

❒ Developed   ❒ Prepared

❒ Evaluated   ❒ Processed

❒ Executed   ❒ Reconciled

❒ Forecasted   ❒ Reviewed

❒ Generated   ❒ Supervised

❒ Identified

The Importance of Accomplishments

The key to creating a rock-solid resume is including bullets that attest to your responsibilities and accomplishments. In turn, these bullets will serve as talking points during your interview, so you can illustrate them with examples. Because your resume will evolve and transform over the years as you color it with new work experiences, you have every right to update your resume. Yes, this means you should update it even when you're looking for a new job. This way, the fluid document will consistently be ready for circulation and you won't go into panic mode when you hit the "oh-my-gah, get-me-outta-here" button. Plus, it's always more challenging looking back on a job you did the past year to recall various projects and accomplishments instead of simply adding to the resume as they happen.

Don't Forget the Cover Letter

Now that you're getting the gist of the whole resume thing and letting your work experience and skill set speak for itself, let's pause out of respect for its little sis, who's often overshadowed. That's right, I said overshadowed. A resume is not complete without a cover letter. You'll always need to submit a cover letter along with your resume. Even when you're applying for jobs through a company's online job postings, you should have a cover letter handy.

The beauty about cover letters is their brevity. They're succinct and to-the-point. You'll state who you are and why you're ideal for the position. Think about it as your elevator speech, except this one's in writing.

Here's a sample cover letter.

Your Address
Your City, State, ZIP Code
Your Phone Number
Your E-mail Address

Date

Name
Title
Organization
Address
City, State, ZIP Code

Dear Mr./Ms. Last Name:

I am very interested in pursuing the human resources coordinator position advertised on Monster.com. I am convinced that my internship experiences as a human resources professional at MTV and IBM, along with my excellent organizational and interpersonal skills, make me a viable candidate for this position.

Thank you for your consideration. I look forward to hearing from you soon.

Sincerely,

Gotham Goddess

Getting Focused

Okay, now that your resume and cover letter are out of the way, you're well on your way to job superstardom. Now you'll need to get some focus, darlin'.

What Was Your Major?

So, that said, what was your major? What color is your parachute? (Seriously, go read that book if you haven't done so already.) For instance, if you were a psychology major, career paths that may be interesting to you could include human resources, social work, and teaching. Assuming that you're not on the grad school route, we'll focus on human resources. But that's not to say you can't get into public relations with a psych degree—or become a paralegal with a psych degree. Truth be told, your major can help you if it's in perfect alignment with a job or industry you're pursuing, but it's definitely not the end-all, be-all.

What Past Experience and Skills Excite You?

This is where the internship is key. Did you have past internships that got you excited? Were there specific skill sets that got you juiced? For instance, if you worked in marketing for a team on the WNBA, maybe you really liked marketing. Perhaps you detested it but there were specific skills that you enjoyed, like being on the phones. This is what I'm sayin'. You need to narrow down your search a tiny bit so that you come up with a list. Not just any list, mind you. This list will include industries. Sure, they can overlap, such that marketing can overlap with public relations can overlap with sales. Or it'll be specific like hedge funds and nothing else.

What Companies Would You Like to Work For?

Next on the list will be companies. You'll need an open mind because there will be companies you've never even heard of, so you may just want to start with the biggies. If you're into cosmetics and marketing, why not try L'Oreal? If you love the Internet, how about Facebook? They do list job openings on their site for Manhattan, you know.

While you're working on the list, you may also want to think about the type of company you want to work for. Do you want to wear jeans to work, or suits? Do you want to be in a laidback environment, or do you thrive in a place that's more conservative? Granted, right out of school you may be open to any environment and that's totally cool. If, however, you can recall an internship that rocked your world (maybe the job itself was kinda sucky but the place was uber cool), write it down.

It's Good to Dream, But...

Tough love segment coming straight at ya. After you get a job, it's very hard to have all facets of your job synergize into a happy-happy, joy-joy type of place. You may absolutely jump out of bed every morning to go to a job you love doing. But your boss may be a miserable wretch who doesn't give you opportunities to shine. Or you may have an amazing boss who reminds you of the best professor you had on campus—you know, the one who challenges you and pushes you to think outside the box to your fullest potential. Guess what? The job may be B to the ORING. You may love the environment but find your co-workers a bit gossipy. Or your co-workers may be super fly but you may hate the commute.

See what I'm saying? Making a list will help narrow down where to start the job search (flexibility is key because you may need to rework that list from time to time) so that it's not so overwhelming. Being realistic, however, is the main thing to keep in mind. Hopefully the positive will outweigh the negative.

And, you won't be married to your job, either. If you find out that your boss has a psychological disorder and makes your life miserable, then yes it's time to move on. If you become bored, master your job, and lack any new challenges, it's time for a promotion or a new gig altogether. The skills I'm bestowing upon you will help you land the next job and the next and the next. But if you're not good on your first one, it'll be harder to get your next.

As you devour the skinny on job stuff, just remember to be flexible and that your first job is not the end-all, be-all.

Figure It Out and then Stick to Your Story

Now that you've created a sense of structure about what you're going after, remember to be clear about your interests and throw in a dash of flexibility. If you want to pursue a job in public relations, there are several industries you could explore, like health care, luxury goods, or entertainment. On the flip side, if you want to pursue a specific industry like entertainment, you can look into opportunities in terms of acting, talent search, marketing, advertising, human resources, finance, and more. Keep in mind that your goals can be fluid as you conduct your job search. But when the inner exploration is done, it's time to get out there and create your destiny!

Where to Start

As you manifest new magic, think about your job search like a beautiful diamond—multi-faceted and brilliant at every angle. Every avenue you explore will provide clarity and illumination during your journey. Whether you work the room at a job fair, speak with an employment agency, create your online strategy, join a job search group or attend industry events, it's all good.

Job Fairs

The first item to add to your to-do list is job fairs! In some cities it may feel like a huge cattle call, but one way to get your foot in the door is to perhaps attend a fair in NYC or go to a local one in your 'hood at home that will have employers with an office in New York City. This way, you'll get to practice your elevator pitch, dress up in a corporate costume (that is, the interview suit), and put in face time with a—get this—live person! Woo-hoo! For instance, if you go to a Women for Hire job fair, you'll know ahead of time which employers will attend by perusing the Web site (www.womenforhire.com). You can certainly do your homework by studying up on the companies that will be there. And don't forget to bring your resume.

Oh yeah, you'll need to attend the job fair as a polished professional. Even if you plan on going to the gym afterward, dress to impress as if you have a job interview at the job fair itself. As for companies that don't have openings but are ultra cool, be bold. Introduce yourself to the recruiter and ask for his or her contact information to follow up.

The more you get out there, the more opportunities you can create for yourself.

Employment Agencies: Job Fairy Godmothers?

Let's not overlook the power of employment agencies. Are they job fairy godmothers? Perhaps. Will they wave a wand and make an awesome job magically appear? Not likely, oh naïve one. What they will do, however, is help you if you select the right one. For instance, an agency will become your advocate and push for you at a certain organization. They'll prep you for the interview and debrief you afterwards. And when an offer is made, guess what? They'll negotiate for you, too. Sounds like a win–win, right? They get paid a percentage of your salary as a commission; notice I didn't say *from* your salary. This means it's not a cut from your pay; rather, it's a cut from the company itself. It's completely separate. By getting a higher salary for you, more moolah ends up in their pocket!

Create Your NYC Brand

According to David Ciliberto—an independent consultant under David Ciliberto Enterprises focusing on human resources, outplacement, coaching, training, and development—you can start playing the New York part by establishing your contact information.

Get a NYC area code (as in 212, 646, or 917). "If you're relocating, I would put contact information as your e-mail address and cell phone number. People pay attention to the first three digits of a phone number with area code." If employers see an out-of-state number, they may immediately say, "I don't want to pay relocation," and move on from your resume. In order to get a coveted NYC area code, speak to your wireless carrier. They may not always be able to hook you up, but if you explain the situation and how you'll have a NYC address soon and want the new digits to reflect your Gotham gal status, they may be quick to oblige. It doesn't hurt to ask.

Change your e-mail address to include your name. Yes, this means GoGirl81@gmail.com should be out of commission, at least when it comes to sending resumes. "Any kind of e-mail with your name included is always a positive way to do it. You don't want someone to forget who you are based on your resume." Your name is a surefire way to create recognition and have potential employers remember you. If your e-mail address is not associated with anything other than fluff, it's certainly one way to be overlooked as your e-mail arrives in a hiring manager's in-box.

Alane Baranello, principal of Alane Baranello and Associates, says you can find an agency through someone with whom you have a connection. "It's good to go with someone who has a specialty because they'll probably know more people." Signing up with a few agencies won't hurt you in your job search. Quite the contrary, it will only help you. Alane recommends perhaps going with three or four, but for entry-level positions, many companies prefer to find talent on their own. Reading between the lines, of course, they don't want to pay the agency fee when there's an abundance of talent on the market.

Since companies aren't using agencies for the most part for entry-level jobs, you need to log onto the job boards, apply to positions, and network a lot. Actually, agencies should tell you up front if they're unable to help you so as to not waste anyone's time. That said, if you want a job in public relations as an assistant, many agencies may not be able to help you. However, if you have a specialty or perhaps even an MBA and did a fast-track program at your school, a well-connected agency may be able to help you.

The process of signing on with an agency is pretty darn simple. You'll be asked to submit your resume. Assuming it passes muster, you'll have an interview over the phone (called a phone screen) with the agency. Alane notes, "If there was a position immediately available you would go further than that, but a lot of agencies don't even bother to meet the person face to face if it's a low-level job."

Remember, the agency is representing you, the talent, yet they're essentially being paid by the client. So guess who they're really working for? The client company. The agency's name and reputation is always being put forth to the client; so while they'll push your resume and candidacy forward in the process, it all reflects upon the agency. So if you do not look like the right candidate for the job, it's in their best interest not to push you.

Taking the Edge Off

Looking for a job in a new city can be intense and downright draining if you let it be. So don't let it consume you, alright? Go for a walk outside. Step away from the computer. How about treating yourself to flowers or a fruit smoothie every now and then? Take care of yourself, whether that means going to the gym, volunteering, or getting a weekly mani/ pedi.

As you're searching for agencies, ask them how they conduct their business. For instance, do they think they can place you or send you out on an immediate interview? "Most agencies don't tend to build that type of relationship, and that's unfortunate when that happens," Alane says.

If your agency is like Alane's, you'll receive background information on the company and the position. In fact, a good agency will help prepare you for the interview so you'll be sure to put your best foot forward. That said, don't rely completely on the agency. You'll still need to do your homework and concoct a few questions, but the agency can help color it with details and information you wouldn't normally have going into the process. "Don't depend on the third party to provide you with all the information you need," she advises. "You still need to become prepared for the interview."

The follow-up process with an agency is the same as you'd adhere to when interviewing directly with companies. Thank-you e-mails? Check. Debrief yourself? Check. Take a deep breath? Check, check, check. In fact, in the case of the agency, it's in your best interest to send them a thank-you note e-mail; you'll want to thank them for their time in prepping you as well as for submitting your resume. If this job doesn't have your name on it, perhaps the agency can help you with another one. Therefore, you'll need to build a relationship with the third party. In any event, job fairs and agents can assist you in terms of getting in touch directly with recruiters. You can get a pulse on the marketplace and make your initial connections.

Set Your Online Strategy

Job fair? Check. Agency? Check. Online job search? Click that mouse and get ready to rumble. This one is so basic that everyone is doing it, which is why you need to devote as little time to possible to it.

Granted, I'm not saying you shouldn't surf company Web sites or job boards and that you should ignore them if you see a promising position. But just know that this step takes minimal effort. The lack of effort required equates to a large number of people having access to it and submitting their resumes. So your odds of landing a job this way are poor.

For the inside scoop, here's what really happens when you submit a resume. It goes into a black hole! (Kidding, of course. That's just the rumor.) What really happens when you apply online through a company Web site is twofold:

✦ Your resume lands in a database and is associated with the specific position you applied to.

✦ Your resume also goes into an "open" database, so the recruiter can find it in the system for future positions, too.

Show Me the Money!

What makes New York special? If you have no clue what you want to do in New York but just know you need to get there, you might as well focus on available opportunities instead of industries that are shrinking (like the print media). Hotspots right now include travel services, the tourism industry, security, health care, and financial services. Plus,

(CONTINUED)

there are peculiarities specific to Gotham like opportunities in the theater, ballet, and yes, bartending.

Although you may be thinking about NYC in terms of its bright lights and all things that glitter, it's also a college town. Between New York University, Columbia University, Fordham, Baruch, Manhattan College, and more, the countless schools need to hire people in a variety of areas such as finance, human resources, and alumni relations. They typically post job openings on their Web sites. One major benefit of working on campus is perks like tuition discounts or free tuition altogether. This, my friend, could be your ticket to living in Manhattan while earning an advanced degree if you desire it. Bonus!

Let's look at the data, shall we? Keep in mind when you look at numbers, it's not all black and white. Sometimes there's a nice shade of gray; data can be deceiving and exceptions exist. According to the U.S. Department of Labor's data from the Occupational Employment Surveys (May 2008), the median wage in the New York/Northern New Jersey/ Long Island/NJ/PA metropolitan area for all occupations is...wait for it...$40,280. Considering that the median wage for all occupations nationally is $32,390, wages in the New York metro area are inflated by 24.4 percent.

Taking a closer look, for instance, salaries may be deceiving based on that equation. Costume attendants may sound like a random occupation, but in New York they are an integral part of the theatre industry. According to the data, the national median wage for this occupation is $26,250. If you simply assume wages in New York are inflated by 24.4 percent, you'll expect the metro's wage to be $32,644. But the wage in New York is actually $57,230, meaning they're inflated to 175.3 percent of their expected wage. Now, that's what I would call an anomaly!

To check out the data for additional knowledge, be sure to log onto the Department of Labor's Web site (www. dol.gov). In addition, the government's Bureau of Labor Statistics' *Occupational Outlook Handbook* (www.bls.gov/oco) has copious amounts of information regarding specific jobs, education requirements, and median wages.

Depending on the specific online system, HR recruiters can look up the specific job; or they may get pinged in their box and will see your resume. Your CV may be surrounded by hundreds of other fine-looking, qualified resumes. Although the internal recruiter may be able to physically parse through all of them or do keyword searches to see whose stands out among the pack, you'll need to get it on someone's desk to forward it to the internal HR team in order to get that call you want.

Considering that many companies have lucrative employee referral programs, when you start connecting with folks you may want to be so bold as to say, "I'm not sure if your company has an employee referral program, but considering that I want to pursue an opportunity here, perhaps it would be helpful for you to submit it? This way, I know my resume will land on someone's desk and you'll be compensated for your efforts." Money talks, babe.

The Case for an MBA

At this point you may be thinking, "hmmm, not quite sure if the long-distance job search is for me." I'm telling you, it is. You'd have to do the job search anyway, right? Why not launch a career in the most spectacular city ever? Well, if I haven't convinced you yet, there is another way in. It's called graduate school.

Personally, I'm not a fan of graduate school just for the sake of going. Why spend the time and money if you're not going to learn and it's not going to push you to the next level, you

(CONTINUED)

(CONTINUED)

know? Well, if your goals are specific and there's job security in obtaining a master's degree, go for it. By that, I don't recommend going for your advanced degree in organizational psychology just because you think it's interesting. However, if you're pursuing your MBA in finance because you want to pursue a statistical valuation position that typically requires an MBA for employment, by all means, do it!

Anyway, if you enroll in a higher-ed program in New York City or the vicinity, that's certainly one way to get here. As you're here, you can perhaps land a part-time job at your local gym or in your neighborhood, which will give you the opportunity to establish your roots and network as much as you can.

Start a Job Search Group

As you're thinking creatively to manifest connections—and more importantly, job opps—why not start a job search group? It'll get you out of the house and connect you with like-minded people with similar goals. You can create one in your hometown easily by posting a listing on craigslist (www.craigslist.org), and start meeting on a weekly basis. It's helpful to have a sounding board and motivation. Plus, as you'll notice, the word "networking" is sprinkled throughout this book. It's a fantastic way to tap into others' job search networks. You'll be able to pool your information resources.

And if you're one of those people who likes to hoard your information and contacts, get over it. You're all in the same boat. Would you want someone withholding an awesome contact for you in the big city? Didn't think so. Plus, if you think members of the group will be competition for your job pursuits, get over it. You each bring unique skills and experiences to the table.

Hey, your energy and passion for New York City is second to none! That will come across to interviewers and your fellow job searchers in the group. They'll want to help you if you want to help them. You can conduct mock interviews with each other or even dish about questions that stumped you in an interview. The more information and connections you share, the better off everyone is. You're in this together. Even though it may feel like you're doing it alone at times, it shouldn't. Rely on people if for no other reason than to give you a diversion from your task. Yes, that means also having friends to hang out with and get your mind off the game!

So Many Choices, So Little Time

New York City is a very big place, and don't you ever forget it. It's so broad and full of opportunities, the only thing you have to do is identify and capitalize on them.

You could work in any function (like public relations) and have a variety of industry choices available to you (like consumer products, luxury goods, fashion, law, entertainment, financial services, and pharmaceuticals).

Join Industry Events and Organizations

Another search strategy involves attending industry events or professional organizations. For instance, the Society for Human Resource Management is a national organization for HR professionals. The ideal strategy would be to continuously attend monthly events in NYC. You'll put in face time, people will begin recognizing you, you can volunteer to work the registration desk in order to meet everyone, and you can ask who they know that is hiring.

If you aren't in the Manhattan vicinity to access local events, never fear. Most organizations have events in various cities throughout the country. The most convenient action item is to attend the one closest to your home and start workin' the room! You may stand out because not everyone there will be looking to relocate to Gotham. Plus, you'll be surprised how many people will want to help you—that is, if they know you are open to receiving the help. You'll need to get past your ego and speak up:

Hi. I'm excited about my job search in Manhattan but I don't seem to know anyone in HR. Is there anyone you recommend I speak to for an informational interview? I'm excited to get into marketing. I earned my degree in marketing and communications and I'm looking specifically to work in the digital marketing space for a Fortune 500 company in Manhattan.

That, my friend, is an elevator pitch. You'll state who you are, what you're looking for, and where you want to do it. Sounds simple, right? You may fumble with your words in the beginning, but that's what friends are for. Practice them, silly. And if you're on the phone, you can always write it down and read from it.

Networking Works Wonders: All. The. Time.

Related to the idea of ask and you shall receive, you might as well have others be your ambassadors, too. Enlist your connections to help you achieve your goal. Go ahead, don't be shy! Make sure they ask around and are open to helping you on your behalf.

For example, Harris Trock, a recent college grad from Cornell University, earned his business degree in the college of agriculture and life sciences. The ink was barely dry on his diploma when he started his new job in the middle of a recession. His father knew someone who worked in New York City and told him what type of work his son was seeking—and behold, a job offer followed. Of course, I'm leaving out the juicy details. Even though his father asked and received a connection, Harris did the rest of the work. Just because you have a solid network (yes, by all means tap into your parents and siblings for help) doesn't mean a job is going to be yours. Harris had to interview and then land the job all on his own.

Harris works in Westchester, which is in New York and is a commutable suburb to Manhattan. The beauty of it is that by working as a financial analyst for a renewable investment energy project, he knows for sure that NYC is available to him; but right now he's staying put.

See chapter 2 for much more on offline and online networking.

Managing the 'Rents

You know they love you, they truly do. You may not even realize how over-involved they're becoming in your search, though. Although some parents may know where to draw the line in terms of helping you via networking, this simply must be addressed. Yes, I'm talking about the hovering and smothering helicopter parent. It's certainly one thing for them to become overly engrossed in your search. It's quite another for them to make it public.

Parents have called recruiters on their kid's behalf. Do they think they're really helping? (And if you're a parent reading this book on behalf of your aspiring New Yorker offspring, oh my, my, my.)

In order to handle them, perhaps explain to them that their phone call is only hurting your shot at being taken seriously by the potential employer. In some instances they may call to find out why you weren't selected for the interview. (By the way, if companies explained why you weren't selected, this could open them up for a potential lawsuit. They don't owe you a reason. Move on.) In other scenarios they may try to negotiate salary on your behalf.

Because they clearly want to see you succeed, why not enlist their services for other endeavors? Tap into their network or perhaps have them call people they know to get referrals for you.

"I kinda got lucky. I didn't have to push things," Harris says. Well, you can guess what happened next.

Soon after he became settled in his new job, Harris got a call from a former internship employer in the form of a potential job offer. While he enjoys living at home and saving tons of money with a three-minute drive to work, avoiding the trains and subways his fellow Cornellians are getting accustomed to, he knows his solid resume of internship experiences, along with his skills, may help him land in the heart of New York City at some point if he chooses to work in the city. His former jobs include marketing for a popcorn company, doing real estate for a global services company, and a distribution job for fruits and vegetables. "Learn how to relate those skills in aspects you're looking for in a job out in the real world." Harris became self-sufficient in terms of going after his goals. Did he leverage his parents' resources? You bet.

Did they hover and smother to the point where they were zooming in on his turf? No way.

So, my dear, what can we learn from Harris aside from the points already mentioned? Resources were abundant in terms of his job search if his current opportunity didn't manifest itself. His career office developed a Facebook group for alums. In addition, another resource is the ability to tap into his career advisor on campus. Plus, he can also connect with alums on a national basis from his fraternity, Sigma Alpha Epsilon.

Transfer Internally

If you end up with a job that's perhaps not located in Manhattan, similar to Harris' situation, maybe you'll luck out and your company's office headquarters will be located in New York. As you pursue jobs, one concept is to always keep the end in mind, realizing that your destination isn't as far away as you think it is. Maybe you have student loans and you're ready for Manhattan, but your bank account isn't? One idea (and I'm just throwing it out there for you to put NYC on the top of your mind within the next 12 months or so) is to consider a job close to your home that has an office in or around Manhattan.

I heart this strategy, I truly do. It's near and dear to my heart, in fact! Maybe that's 'cuz I did it successfully and you can, too. Repeat these two pretty little words after me: internal transfer. Just take it from Valentina Afanasii, a senior associate at KPMG LLP. Valentina has her MBA in accounting and worked for the accounting firm for two years in Shreveport, Louisiana, before relocating to the Big Apple. "I wanted to try something new while growing my career at KPMG," she says. In fact, she originally chose KPMG as an employer for the variety of opportunities it offered. As such, she identified international tax as a field to better fit her background. After talking to her home office partner about the internal transfer, she got the green light to move ahead.

By having already worked for the global firm, Valentina's move sounded seamless. "KPMG is KPMG regardless. Deadlines are deadlines. The work is almost the same and the pace is just as intense here as it is anywhere else." She found there was always someone available to help. For instance, Valentina found her city apartment through friends of a friend of a friend. Her goal is to live in Manhattan for a few years and then perhaps later move to another area and commute to the midtown office.

If the concept of transferring internally sounds enticing, listen up: You typically have to be a strong performer at home. You can't produce mediocre work and then expect your boss to be on board with your idea. There are a few other caveats as to why it may not work. Your original company may be small and might not have an office in New York (no brainer). However, perhaps you can ask your company for the opportunity to telecommute; and in this case, it won't matter where your home office is located.

The best way to do it is two-fold: I found the opportunity and pursued it. Living in New Jersey, I was isolated and bored to tears (I kid you not, it was truly stifling; it was certainly time to move on). Moving internally had its major advantages: By staying with the same company you don't have the added stress of taking on a brand-new corporate culture. Although my job itself was new, the company naturally remained the same, as did my contacts at home. Even something as cumbersome as connecting to a new server was relatively stress-free because the 800 number for the help desk had not changed, nor did the process for opening a ticket and navigating the internal network drives.

In the case like Valentina's, she created the opportunity. Because she had already obtained the proper skill set and the field she wanted to pursue already existed, the partners realized the need for her talent in New York City. If you have the bright idea to create an opportunity that doesn't exist, lo and behold, you will be very disappointed. But, if you have the wherewithal to say hey, NYC is for me and my performance is better suited in this type of job, and you have got a stellar reputation to back you up, all the better!

Think of it this way instead: The company isn't really taking a risk on you because you've already proved yourself at home. Now, I'm not saying it's okay to become a total slacker after you move. You've got to keep up your performance at the new location as well.

The reverse is true as well. Let's say you absolutely love your job in New York but you're ready to think even bigger. International, perhaps? Go get 'em! You've proven yourself in New Yawk for a few years and noticed your company has a job opening for a related position in marketing in Amsterdam. My advice? Go for it! You can leverage your skill set and experience with the company toward the opportunity for which you're qualified.

Depending on the industry and your specific job, an overseas stint may help catapult your career in the long term. You can demonstrate how you've worked cross-culturally and gained new skills. It will give you an edge over other candidates without international experience when you're gunning for the same job. Plus, if you have honed your language skills, your global experience could be an asset to your resume.

Or perhaps you want to pursue your MBA near your hometown. You might be able to transfer to your hometown's office, either doing the same job or with reduced hours, so that you can pursue your MBA, then leave within three or four years. It's not a bad idea to start thinking about your long-term goals and how your current job will help get you there.

That's a Wrap

Get the drift of this chapter? It's all about thinking outside the cubicle. As your career goddess in Gotham, I simply must remind you to take the reins of your career and propel yourself forward. Job fairs, local associations, agencies, landing with a company with NYC ties—it's all good.

I will outline additional strategies in other chapters, along with networking tips. When you combine them all into a holistic approach to the job search, you, too, will come out a survivor. And by that I mean happily employed in New York.

Takeout: Resources to Go

Web Sites

craigslist: www.craigslist.org

U.S. Department of Labor: www.dol.gov

U.S. Department of Labor Bureau of Labor Statistics: www.bls.gov/oco

Women for Hire: www.womenforhire.com

Books

What Color Is Your Parachute? (Richard N. Bolles)

CHAPTER 2

GO TIME: ONLINE AND OFFLINE NETWORKING

While there are certainly several ways to get a foot in the door, one sure way to make huge strides toward your goal is to network. As in *work the room. Work it. Make it work.* However you want to say it, you'll be doing a lot of it. Essentially, the importance of your communication skills just got kicked up 10 notches because you'll be speaking, writing, and e-mailing frequently.

Although networking technically goes both ways and you'll certainly be able to help others, too, for the purposes of this chapter it's all about you! Yes, this means you're the star of your own show, so don't let me down, 'k?

Offline Networking

You need to start from the very beginning: figuring out who your network is. Then I'll break it down to the two-pronged approach of sitting behind your computer and then literally getting out there. You'll need to either get a notebook or start a spreadsheet in Excel—whatever you prefer. Ready? Let's go!

Make Your List of Contacts

Crank up some fun tunes and start a game of free association. Start with your friends. Write down all of their names, even people who are your Facebook friends but not your friends in real life (you know what I mean). Okay, next is their parents. Maybe you met some of their parents at various school functions? Write them down, too. How about professors on campus? Any alums you met at various events? How about organizations you belonged to, like an honor society or sorority? What about the basics like your parents, their friends, your neighbors, and your siblings? Let's dive a little deeper, shall we? (Do you have a choice?) How about your manicurist, hairstylist, pool guy, cable guy, and personal trainer? Seriously.

By now your list should have at least 20, if not 30, names on it. I think it's important to celebrate little milestones in the process, so let's pause for a second:

Go, you!

Okay, moving on. That was a nice moment and a huge step as you're laying the foundation of your network brick by brick. You'll never have to do this exercise again, by the way, because your network will continue to grow as long as you maintain it. None of this should feel painful because let's remember: Your job search is a par-tay! This is precisely why you need to listen to cool music as you think of anyone and everyone you know. They will help you and you'll need to reach out to them. If you're shy, I have three little words for you: Get over it. The more you strides you make in connecting with people, the more comfortable you will become in putting yourself out there.

Work It!

Rachel Nelson Moeller, an Associate Director of Career Services at Lafayette College (Easton, Pennsylvania), says you must, must, must get out there.

Talk about your goals and realize that everyone is a connection to your coveted life in New York. "Maybe your hairdresser has a connection for you, or maybe it's the lady that's always on the treadmill next to you at the gym. Do anything you can, short of wearing a sandwich board around the neighborhood, to communicate with those who can help you. Regional college alumni chapter groups are a great option for this."

"Young adults need to get out from their computers to do an effective job search. Go out to events, network in person, call people on the phone, follow up on applications, do informational interviews in person or on the phone, etc. Spending all day on electronic job boards WILL NOT land you a job. Yes, online postings are a part of the process, as are online networking sites like LinkedIn. But they are no substitute for in-person exchanges," says Rachel.

Get Their Deets

Moving on. Okay, you've created your first list of everyone you know. The next step is documenting contact information for their digits and e-mail addresses. You'll want to start reaching out to them and setting daily goals for doing that. How about contacting five people each day? Within a week you should be able to bang through the preliminary list. And in two weeks you'll follow up.

Make Contact

Don't start off your networking with a spiel like, "Hi, I'm Andrea's friend and she mentioned I can talk to you about possible jobs in advertising." That's a no-no-no. Mainly you want to focus on the New York job search. Your first goal is to reach out to your contact and ensure that you not only talk about jobs, you talk about jobs in New York. Keep in mind that I'm assuming you don't live near Manhattan or know anyone there. But if you have contacts who already do business there, or if you're already living in a nearby location like Connecticut or something, you'll change your approach.

This approach is not one-size-fits-all, but rather a "hey, it'll fit most people." Tweak it as necessary. Actually, you'll need to revise your approach as you proceed to see what's working and not working.

The first method of communication is typically an e-mail. This way you're not being intrusive with someone or interrupting them when they've just eaten a meal or attended a bad meeting. Of course, if you know the connection personally (like it's your cousin or something), feel free to call and catch up with him or her! For the most part, though, e-mail will work best, assuming it's a connection you're not too close with.

Here's a sample of a networking e-mail that you might send:

Dear Rich,

Hello! I received your contact information from your neighbor, Joe Brown. He mentioned that you have an extensive background in working in the financial markets in Manhattan.

Although I'm currently based in Chicago, I'm seeking to relocate to New York and would love to pursue a position on Wall Street. Would it be possible for us to schedule a 20-minute phone call within the next two weeks to hear about any advice you may have to break in? Since I'm conducting a long-distance job search, I would greatly appreciate any insight you have to offer.

Thank you for your time. I look forward to hearing from you soon.

Best,

Gotham Goddess

Although e-mail is typically the first mode of communication you'll use, it'll be the second as well because you can always forward the initial message to follow up. That said, placing a call to follow up doesn't hurt, either, because e-mails often get buried in overflowing inboxes.

The next step is the phone call. This is where the fun begins! Who doesn't love to talk? You might discover that you're connected to the contact in a unique way. (Maybe you grew up in the same town? Maybe you both have a passion for the same baseball team?) Anyway, try to schedule a time to speak to the person so that you're not playing phone tag for weeks on end.

When you get the person on the phone, be sure to take notes and truly listen to what he's saying. Sometimes you may get so incredibly focused on asking the questions you've already written down ahead of time that you forget to listen to cues. For instance, if the person starts rambling on about a mentor he had, why not ask if you can reach out to that mentor? Although you may have prewritten questions as you interject some of the ones in this chapter, you're not a robot!

Sample Questions

Here are some questions you can ask your contact:

✦ How did you break into your field?

✦ How did you get to where you are today?

✦ What were some skills/experiences that helped you get that job?

✦ What would you do if you were in my position?

✦ What does your company base hiring decisions on?

✦ What skill set should I add to my resume or perhaps hone in order to ensure I'll be considered when a position opens up?

✦ What are some professional organizations I should join?

✦ Do you have suggestions perhaps as to who I should contact within your company?

✦ Do you have any contacts in Manhattan that I can talk to, just as a buddy, as it relates to housing or to have a familiar face when I finally move there?

The phone call should flow like a conversation. Keep it fluid, be yourself, and don't be nervous. This is yet another beautiful aspect to networking. When you're making the initial calls, it's not a job interview, so you can relax. Don't be unprofessional, just relax. Your goal is to make the connection, learn a little information, and most importantly, find out who they know. Most of the time when someone gets a job, it's the result of someone knowing someone knowing someone who knew the boss. In fact, when it happens for you, it probably won't be directly through your network. It'll be through your network's network's network.

All of the e-mails, phone calls, and yes, even coffee meet-ups (completely recommended if the contact has the time) will work wonders. This is where your spreadsheet or notebook comes in handy. Every time you make contact with someone, you should track the date as well

as the information—and most importantly, the new contact information! Here's the thing: Your old contact is always as good as gold. If
they refer you to someone new, reach out to that newbie and then send
a thank-you note to the originator as a note of gratitude.

Right about now you may be thinking all of this networking is work.
Scheduling calls, maintaining a spreadsheet, you gotta be kidding me,
right? Well, it is work somewhat, but it's also part of the ticket to your
new life. Still complaining now?

Expanding Your Network Further

We've only just begun to devour this topic! Okay, you'll notice that
the offline networking process is very similar to the online one in that
you reach out to your contact's contacts. So after you nail down the
communication skills, it's time to expand, expand, expand! The free-
association list was certainly a fun task. So now it's time to flex some
creative brain cells. Some networking connections will require more
steps to reach.

Let's say you want to pursue a position in marketing, advertising, or
public relations. Now is the time to reach out to your career services
office on campus, indicate that you're a recent graduate, and ask for an
e-mail directory of their alums in those specific fields within the greater
NYC region. Score! How about doing the same for your other organizations? Of course, you could start with the industry itself while not
focusing on New York City. As you cruise through the process, you'll
notice that your search gets more refined and focused with each contact
you encounter. The time and effort you put forth will begin to generate
results. The more you network, the more you'll begin to see meaningful
dialogue, advice, and connections, leading you closer to your goal.

On the next page is an example of an e-mail you can send to contacts
that your alma mater gives you.

Now you're probably wondering when is it okay to ask your contact
about a job? All the time, silly! You're not going to come right out and
say, "Hire me" or "Can I interview with you?" Rather, you'll be direct
but tactful. Why not ask whether you may connect with the human
resources organization at the person's company to learn more about

his company? Or how about doing more homework (and I must say, I shouldn't even have to mention this, but I will)?

Subject: Networking Via Alumni Office

Dear Debbie,

Hello! The State U. career service office provided me with your contact information. I'm a recent graduate conducting a job search in Manhattan. The office mentioned that you're a marketing director and I'm particularly interested in speaking with you because that was my major area of study.

I wanted to see whether perhaps I may schedule an informational interview with you on the phone within the next two weeks for about 20 minutes? I realize you're busy but I wanted to tap into your knowledge and experience since this is my first foray into the Real World.

In particular, I'd love to hear your insights and advice you may have for me given the industry and NYC market.

I look forward to hearing from you soon. Thank you in advance for your time.

Sincerely,

Gotham Goddess

Do Your Homework

Before you talk to every single person, you should do homework. If you don't have more than five minutes to spare (come on, you're unemployed, you should have all the time in the world!), at the very least you need to review the company's Web site to see whether there are job openings. This, my friend, is a no-brainer. Your phone informational interview or coffee meet-up will be completely different if there is an opportunity available. If there is a job that you want to go for, you need to mention it to your contact, ask whether he could submit your resume to the recruiting department, and get the name of the person he submits it to so that you can follow up. If you're not proactive and micromanaging the process, no one else will be.

How to Maintain Your Contacts

Dave Ciliberto totally keeps up with his contacts by doing some research and reaching out from time to time. For instance, after a contact asked him about Toastmasters (a public speaking organization), he found out about the charter, how much it would cost to open a new one, outlined 15 steps to get chartered, compiled it into his notes, and sent it to his contact.

"They didn't have to do any of the work; I did it for them. Now, it took me a while; but hey, nothing ventured, nothing gained. I made a good impression." His contact is in human resources and who knows when she might call him for an opportunity? And even if she doesn't, Dave generated some goodwill and learned a lot about Toastmasters in the process.

Online Networking

Getting the hang of the whole networking thing? Good, I knew you would. Essentially the most effective networking will eventually happen offline. As in face time. Whether you make an initial connection on LinkedIn or in person at the salon, they will lead to e-mails, and calls, and job offers. Realizing the importance of offline networking, you can't dismiss the fact that the online world exists and can only help you.

We'll start with the obvious: Yes, you should update your Facebook status and send messages to everyone in your friends list who is located in Manhattan. Here's the thing about updating your status: Be succinct but not desperate. Perhaps you can state, "Seeking entry-level advertising job in NYC. Got leads?" You'll need to state what you're looking for in New York and how your friends can help. For instance, is it a job lead you're seeking, or a headhunter's name in Gotham, or simply a connection within a specific industry? Feel free to update it frequently, vary it from week to week, and most importantly, keep it professional.

As you're job hunting, the last thing you want to do is appear unprofessional as you're soliciting your friends for their help. So, if you previously thought nothing about saying how hung over you were from a birthday party, please think twice before revealing too much personal information via your status update. Sometimes you may get a direct hit as a friend may have a job lead or professional connection for you. Other times you may not get anything more than a "like" indicator that one of your pals is supportive of your goals. You may end up with a potential roommate because one of your friends has another friend with goals to also move to Manhattan. Although the outcome of your status updates may vary, by stating precisely what you're seeking, you're traveling in the direction toward your destiny rather than simply standing still.

You can also log onto the Internet to gain access to your alma mater's alumni database (assuming they have one). But the main topic we simply must discuss is LinkedIn (www.LinkedIn.com). Remember this site, bookmark it, and etch it into your brain. It will play a vital role in your search.

LinkedIn

I heart LinkedIn and you will, too. It's a professional networking site. This is worth repeating. It's *professional*. As in no tagging, no photo albums, no wall. So what good is it, you ask? A whole lot. The best way to explain it is that it's like an online resume. You can post your educational background, honors, groups, associations, as well as work experience. You may also include a status update, like "Ashley is seeking employment in public relations or marketing in the greater NYC area."

Creating Your Profile

As you create your profile, feel free to add keywords that you wish you had on your resume. Am I asking you to lie? Nope. Am I asking you to market yourself appropriately? Yes, yes, yes. You can say in the text that you're seeking a position to demonstrate your multitasking skills or ability to manage a product or function. Recruiters actually use this site and search by keywords based on skill set, associations, or companies; so the more you include, the better.

For instance, if you are an aspiring CPA, by all means include it in your profile, along with the year you anticipate sitting for the exam. This shows you mean business. As you update your profile, even after you land that coveted job, keep in mind that anyone can search for you. Typos are a major no-no and you want to almost micromanage the information on your profile.

Making Connections

After your profile is decked out (and by the way, feel free to attach a professional-looking head shot of yourself), let the connections begin! You may notice randoms sending you requests, the same way you get friend requests on Facebook and have no idea who the person is. I typically ignore them and only accept requests from people I know; but hey, that's just me. If that person is in your field, went to your college, or has some other connection to you, it might not hurt to accept.

Start looking up and connecting with people you know. Whether it's a sorority sister, a career advisor on campus, or your economics professor, by all means send them an invite. Start adding groups you want to belong to, like the Step Up Women's Network in New York City or a national group you want to be part of, like Women for Hire. You will receive messages people post within the group and will have the ability to answer them.

Even if you're not actually a member of the group in real life, for the most part it's totally cool to join it. When you want to belong to a group you'll need to request to become a member. The administrator will either approve or deny you. The beauty of groups is becoming in the know. There may be instances where you're rejected, such as perhaps wanting to join a national alumni sorority group. Please use your tactfulness here, sister. If you weren't a member of the sorority on campus, why fudge it? (Then again, not exactly sure how the administrator would know the truth unless he or she verified it with the national home office.) Nevertheless, there are countless groups on LinkedIn. Your job is to figure out which ones are appropriate and relevant to join.

The Kevin Bacon Game

If you haven't heard of the Kevin Bacon Game, what rock have you been living under? Okay, sarcasm aside, it goes something like this: Elisabeth Shue was in *The Karate Kid* with Ralph Macchio, who was in *The Outsiders* with Kevin Bacon. Or how about this one: Val Kilmer was in *Top Gun* with Tom Cruise; Tom was in *A Few Good Men* with Kevin Bacon. The point is this: Everyone is six relationships (or less) separated from Kevin Bacon.

Started as a drinking game by a few guys in '94 at Albright College, the pop culture party game is still going strong. But how does this relate to the job search, you ask?

I challenge you to find a job you really want without knowing someone who knows someone who knows someone who is connected. For real. You will be able to connect with people; and as such, that is how the Real World game will work. You'll connect with a Demi-type who worked with a Drew-type who previously gigged it with an Ashton who met up with a Brad who most certainly knew the CEO, Jack. Got it? The fun of it is you may not know how someone is connected going into it. If someone has a direct connection to the person or company you're trying to reach, fabu! If not, it'll take some work.

This is where LinkedIn comes into play. As soon as you click on someone you don't know, there will be arrows pointing to people in your network who know someone in your network who knows someone who knows someone who knows that certain someone. The mission, should you choose to accept it (and we both know you totally will), is to add people to your network. I guess it's like a game in a way. The more people in your network, the easier it will be to add coveted people to your network and get through to the one person who holds the key to your new job.

With LinkedIn you can write and receive recommendations. This is key; it's almost like having your professor provide feedback on your performance in class for the whole world to see, except now it's in a professional context. Maybe your former internship boss will have a few kind words to say? Or perhaps it will be a professor attesting to your hard work ethic?

Granted, your boss, mentor, professor, or whomever is not a mind reader. Simply ask for recommendations and you shall hopefully receive. Before the recommendation posts to your profile, you'll have the opportunity to review it. Quite honestly, it's a great way to have a sneak peek at the recommendation, but could you imagine going back to the originator and asking him or her to tweak it a little and make it sparkle a little more? Not likely. Anyway, as soon as you approve it, the recommendation will appear on your profile. Oh yeah, it's nice to return the favor and write a positive recommendation as well.

Remember in the offline section when you created a ginormous list of everyone you knew and wanted to connect with? Voilà! If they're on LinkedIn, it's seriously the best way to stay in touch. As they move on to new jobs (and this is why it's key to connect with former internship supervisors), you'll know about it. Plus, the more people you connect with, the more you can tap into your network. As long as they keep their network visible to their connections list, you'll be able to see who they're connected to. From there you'll be able to contact those people directly through InMail or by reaching your first contact, who can then forward your message to the next one. Sometimes there may be a string of more than one person involved, and that's certainly fine, too.

Use LinkedIn for Following Up

You may become an active user on LinkedIn, or you may not. But I would be completely negligent if I didn't fill you in on this site, sistah! If you want to be an uber user (and let's face it: The bigger and more robust your quality network is, the more you can help others, and vice versa), listen up.

As soon as I attend any networking event and exchange business cards, within 24 hours I treat it like a thank-you note from an interview. Yep, I send my new contacts a message! But instead of e-mail, it's via LinkedIn. Sure, I keep a binder of all the business cards I receive. But when it comes to staying in touch, I get on LinkedIn and search for their profile. If they don't have one (boo—shame on them!), I'll send them an e-mail instead. If they are on LinkedIn, I typically send them a request to join my network with a little note like, "It was great meeting you tonight at the media mixer. I enjoyed talking to you about our passion for handbags! Looking forward to staying in touch via LinkedIn."

The 80/20 Rule

Eugenia (Jeannie) Liakaris, Expert Career Coach, PATHS & Women for Hire, and Senior Career Advisor, Baruch College, Zicklin School of Business, says to tell every single person you know what you're doing, where you are in your search, and what your goals are.

"These people include your parents, your siblings, your aunts/uncles, former classmates, colleagues, even mailmen! Leverage your network and get the word out there."

Plus, she says, you should conduct 20 percent of your job search efforts online. Although job boards and online networking are helpful, you should do the remaining 80 percent of your networking offline. If you're finding it difficult to detach from the computer, create a daily plan of being on the computer two hours each day and that's it.

Above all, step away from the computer and network. "Talk to people who work in positions that you're interested in to find out about their career path. How did they get into that role? Say, 'I'd like to get into this area; what do I need to do now to be a better candidate?'"

Keep in mind that when you go to networking events or business functions, it's usually mutually assumed that the other people are open to networking, too. Therefore, sending a request via LinkedIn is not unusual; rather, it's par for the course. Another reason why it's beneficial is that you may lose their business card or contact information. Well, if LinkedIn is connected to their active e-mail address, you can always reach them regardless of whether they change their address. I don't even know some of my colleagues' e-mail addresses anymore (which also happens on Facebook). I simply message them via the social networking site.

The key to LinkedIn is creating a quality network that you can frequently tap into. Every time (as in yes, every single time) I achieve my goal of collecting at least three meaningful business cards at an event, I follow up on LinkedIn—that is, if the new contacts haven't already beat me to it!

Or perhaps another strategy for you is to follow up with a contact after a phone informational interview. By sending a thank-you via LinkedIn, you'll tap into their network as well as express your gratitude.

> **Note:** *Word to the wise: Not everyone is attached at the hip to LinkedIn. Perhaps the e-mail address they used on LinkedIn is defunct, or they rarely check it. For instance, I've sent thank-yous and invites to join my network and received responses months after the fact. If someone doesn't respond right away, that is typically the reason.*

Another idea is to always connect to recruiters on LinkedIn after you speak with them. Whether they're the internal human resources department or a third-party agency, it's all good. As recruiters they're in the business to connect with people; so, as you can probably imagine, their network will likely be big and waiting for you to tap into it!

Summing It Up

Okay, here are a few parting words singing the praises of this professional site: You can search for specific people. Hark, hear the herald angels sing! Using the example of Condé Nast sales, you can input a company, name, location, title—you name it—and voilà! You'll get results. This is particularly helpful if you want to tap into your alumni network because not all campus career offices have current information. By conducting a search through your connections—whether it's your alma mater, sorority, national honor society, you name it—you will have access to people in the location and company where you want to work. Nifty, eh?

Twitter

What would an online networking section be without talking about Twitter? Ah, Twitter, how I adore you, too. If you don't totally get Twitter, this crash course will set you straight.

Twitter is a micro-blogging site on which you'll post updates in 140 characters or less (called tweets). What's the purpose, you ask? Plenty. You can build your network without knowing people. Instead of connecting with contacts based on actual in-person connections like you do on LinkedIn, the landscape changes on Twitter. Actually, you can most definitely connect with people you know, but the beauty is connecting with people you don't know and sharing information.

Your Twitter handle will be @YourName or whatever you want it to be. Remember, in the job search world you're branding yourself, so nothing will be better than simply using your name. As you start gaining followers and people start following you, you can connect with companies. Recruiters. People who will hire you! You can shout it to the world that you have a specific expertise, such as perhaps by linking to a blog post you wrote about the way Dunkin' Donuts markets its coffee. Whatever you want to say, others will hear it loud and clear.

For instance, why not start with a simple tweet like, "NYC or Bust! Seeking employment in financial markets." You'll need to be succinct; and quite honestly, I think that's why I like it so much. You can get your point across in an instant!

Now, since you're going to use Twitter for professional purposes, please don't be that person. Don't let us know that you ate a tuna-fish sandwich for lunch or that it's a beautiful day to start doing bikram yoga. Rather, work the site to your advantage and embrace the connections you're making (yes, you can send direct messages to people as well). Why not connect with a congresswoman or follow a news station? Companies have their own handles (a.k.a. Twitter pages) as do celebrities. And getting back to the topic: Plenty of recruiters are on Twitter.

As you update your status, be aware that it's blasted to your entire network. And if your profile is made public, anyone can log onto www.twitter.com and access your updates. And if someone googles you (as many recruiters do), your Twitter page will come up high in the rankings. Therefore, why not use your status updates to mention that you've made networking calls and you're going to research a professional organization? And oh, if you want to make your page private, don't even bother logging onto the site at all. What's the point? Your goal is to connect with people and get a job in New York. Period.

There have been reports in the news that people have gotten jobs through Twitter, so please don't underestimate the power of a tweet. People can retweet your message and send it out to their contacts—and so on. All the more reason for you to ensure that your grammar is correct and you've spell-checked it not once but twice. Lucky for us, it's only 140 characters long!

That's a Wrap

Networking is critical and essential to your success, not only in your job search but in your life. Seriously, aside from being able to get an interview and job through networking, it's your connection to people. Chances are you'll snag more phone interviews this way than anyway else. Why would a stranger want to talk to you unless the stranger is specifically connected to you via someone else?

For purposes of your search, the contact is helping you and you're seeking information and new contacts to move forward. Let's not forget it works both ways, so be available to help your network, too. And oh yeah, you can call upon your network for all sorts of nifty things like recommendations for a good hairstylist in your soon-to-be New York neighborhood, a way to get coveted U2 tickets when they're in concert, or even a way to meet the man of your dreams (more on that in chapter 11).

Takeout: Resources to Go

Web Sites

LinkedIn: www.linkedin.com

Twitter: www.twitter.com

CHAPTER 3

PATIENCE AND PERSEVERANCE: ATTITUDE IS EVERYTHING

As much as you can be equipped with the nuts and bolts to network like the best of 'em, work a room, circulate that resume, snag informational interviews, ace the real interview, and eventually land a job, if you don't possess an ounce of positivity, you're a fish out of the Hudson River water.

Trust me on this one. While all of the other chapters have discussed tools and tips that will help you get to Gotham, I must pause to discuss the dreaded "r" word. That's right, I'm talking about rejection. Every interview will not result in a job offer, nor will every connection lead to another open door. Therefore, it's important to keep your chin up and keep on keepin' on. You can only get better and better at your interviewing skills and your ability to negotiate with ease. If there's one section of this book you will frequently need to refer to, it might very well be this one.

Every now and then you'll need a little inspiration and empowerment to get you through the search. I never said it would be easy (though I did say it would be fun). At the point where it starts feeling like a chore or you feel frustrated, keep patience and perseverance in mind, alright?

> **Note:** *Oh, if you need to peruse another section for attitudinal inspiration, flip ahead to chapter 11, "Get a Sizzlin' Social Life." Knowing that your magnificent city life beckons your arrival may help you get through some of the slumps of the job search process.*

Embrace Your Individuality

According to Vincent Libretti, the vibrant personality and effervescent talent from the 2006 season of the hit reality show *Project Runway*, if something doesn't feel right, don't force it. He explains, "If something doesn't work, remove it so you create room for something better to come in." Libretti, who still rocks out to designing high-end clothing and has now started designing ergonomic clothing as well as webisodes with Mutiny Pictures, says you must be honest with yourself. "Know who you are and what you would like to do."

As for his advice? Enthusiasm is priceless. And so is individuality. "Individuality is always a good thing to approach opportunities which give you the ability to unveil who you are and what you are." For instance, if you picture yourself as a high-end designer but you truly rock out to sportswear, go with the latter. "You have to listen to what you desire from the inside and follow that dream."

Perseverance Pays Off via Harry Potter

If you're not convinced that you can flip rejections upside down, perhaps you've heard about Joanne "Jo" Murray? If not, perhaps the pen name of J.K. Rowling will ring a bell instead? The British author is known for her rags-to-riches story when she went from living on welfare to achieving multi-millionaire status within five years. The 2008 *Sunday Times* "Rich List" estimated her fortune at almost $800 million!

On a four-hour-delayed train ride from Manchester to London in 1990, J.K. concocted the idea for the Harry Potter fantasy series. It started with Harry, and then all of the characters and situations flooded into her head.

That December her mother died after a 10-year battle with multiple sclerosis. She hadn't had a chance to tell her mother about Harry Potter, but said the death heavily impacted her writing.

After getting married and having a daughter, she was diagnosed with clinical depression and contemplated suicide. This brought about the idea of Dementors, creators lacking souls.

In 1995 she finished off her manuscript, *Harry Potter and the Philosopher's Stone,* on a retro typewriter. She snagged a literary agent, but guess what? Her book was submitted to 12 publishing houses and they all rejected the manuscript. A year later a small British publishing house decided to publish her book since its chairman's eight-year-old daughter was given the first chapter to read and instantly wanted to see a second and third.

Although the publisher agreed to publish the book, Rowling was advised to get a day job since they thought she had little chance of making money on children's books. Of course, we all know how wrong that turned out to be.

As for when things don't go your way—and let's face it, things won't always be on your side—simply surrender. Embrace the defeat and move on quickly. For instance, if you interviewed with a company two weeks ago and haven't heard back yet, following up is fine. But badgering a company or trying too hard will not help you. If anything, it will hurt your candidacy because you'll begin to seem stalker-ish. Instead, let it go and move on to an employer that wants to interview you and consequently follows up with two pretty words: "You're hired."

Libretti explains, "Oftentimes people hold or carry things to push them and want to make it work. If something doesn't feel right, 99 percent of the time it may end up in trouble down the road. Let it go; you'll leave room for something better to come in." For instance, perhaps you're yearning to get your internship experience in advertising noticed by a big agency in the big city. You're holding on, keeping the faith and pushing them, almost forcing them to consider your candidacy. Perhaps the company clearly shut the door and sent rejection notes to you more than once. According to Vincent, it's prudent to simply accept it's not right and let it go. This way, your efforts may be redirected toward another employer that will be more receptive.

And when there's room for new opportunities to enter your life, you'll be ready to embrace them and act in the moment. After all, if you're too busy dwelling on the past or becoming anxious about the future, you'll totally miss the present. It's such a gift, isn't it? In fact, Vincent says the biggest lessons he learned when he was conducting business in New York City pertained to staying in the moment. When you don't stay in the moment and focus on the past or stress about the future, you're actually nowhere. "In New York, I lived in the moment. You have to intend to stay in the moment. This allows creativity to flow. Passion needs this freedom."

Freedom results from letting go. Right about now you're probably wondering in all italics, *"But how will this help land me a job to jump-start my sizzling life in the city?"* Career karma is the end-all and be-all. You can have the nuts and bolts to land a job and interview your way to the corner cubicle, but if you don't have the ability to see the big picture, you'll be nowhere. Just take it from Steve Jobs.

"Trust the Dots Will Somehow Connect"

The beauty of life sometimes lies within not knowing the answers or results while you're entrenched in pondering the questions themselves. Sounds deep, yes? It's true. As you forge ahead to gain a new skill or even pursue a new hobby, you'll never know when you'll be able to apply your new insight or talents down the road.

Perhaps you've heard of Steve Jobs, the co-founder and CEO of Apple, Inc., and former CEO of Pixar Animation Studios? Well, he was originally a student at Reed College before he dropped out. He couldn't figure out why he should spend all of his working-class parents' life savings on an education with which he had no idea what he wanted to do, and he trusted everything was going to work out just fine.

As for the kicker? As soon as Steve dropped out, he stopped taking all of the required classes that didn't interest him. The upside, of course, was that he started dropping in on ones that looked interesting and intriguing, like calligraphy. He learned about serif and san serif type-faces, varying the amount of space between letter combos, and he found it downright fascinating. So, if you're feeling somewhat down and out and wondering how you'll ever use your degree in the real world, let alone some of the lesser-known courses you took on campus, listen up because the story gets better.

> **Note:** *If you think I'm trying to say that dropping out of college is the message here, you're so missing the point! It's all about going with your gut, doing things for the sake of enjoyment, and realizing that it will all make better sense in retrospect, even if it doesn't make any sense in the moment.*

The story continues: Ten years later when they were designing the first Macintosh computer, it all came back to him. They designed what he learned about calligraphy into the Mac! If Steve hadn't dropped into that course, the Mac would not have multiple typefaces or proportion-ally spaced fonts. Since Windows simply copied the Mac, its programs have them, too. In a commencement speech at Stanford University in 2005, Steve mentioned that if he had never dropped out, he never would have dropped in on the calligraphy class and personal computers might not have the typography they do today.

"Of course it was impossible to connect the dots looking forward when I was in college. But it was very, very clear looking backwards 10 years later. Again, you can't connect the dots looking forward; you can only connect them looking backwards. So you have to trust that the dots will somehow connect in your future. You have to trust in something—your gut, destiny, life, karma, whatever. This approach has never let me down, and it has made all the difference in my life."

Advice from the *Project Runway* Alum

The ego, notes Vincent, should be left at the door. "It can get in anyone's way. People who get ahead don't display this enormous ego. The willingness to surrender is the most profitable guide to success."

Getting "in" takes persistence to get past the gatekeepers (that is, receptionists). If you make them feel good and you're energetic, they will help you.

"Stick to what and who you are and sooner or later if you don't give up, you will succeed. Persistence is the package. You mix it with a little humility and a lot of enthusiasm; it's a formula for success!"

Clear Goals Produce Clear Results

To really drive the point home, let's check in with Jennifer Macaluso-Gilmore. She's a coach and the founder of Something Different for Women, a series of inspirational courses for females. By starting with the end in mind, you know for sure what your goal is, in case you ever forget: big job, big life in the Big Apple. Has anything ever not worked out for you the way you wanted it to? Remember when you were in high school stressing beyond belief about those darn SATs? And how about college applications and essays? Well that turned out pretty okay, didn't it? Deep breaths darlin', deep breaths.

Assuming everything up to this point has worked out just the way it was meant to, you have no reason to believe your job search won't, either. Now, get ready to get truly specific and strike up the band! Jen says first and foremost, hazy goals produce hazy results. Be specific and get really clear.

"The clearer you are about your intention, the more likely you are to achieve the desired outcome," she says. While we're on the topic, what *is* your intention? Let's get specific, shall we? Is it to get a great job doing something you absolutely love to do? Is your goal to make enough money to cover your bills and then some? Is it to get any ol' job to allow you to afford living in NYC? Is it to break into a difficult industry and start from the bottom up? She adds, "If you don't have a clear intention, you'll spread yourself thin."

Take a Break When You Need One

Which brings up the next topic: the tailspin! Suppose you sent out 15 cover letters this week and made five follow-up calls from last week, and then you're surfing for jobs one hour uninterrupted (as in no Facebook or YouTube, go you!). So why, oh why, aren't you seeing results? This, my friend, is not where you start bashing your head against the wall or breaking out the supersized dark chocolate bar from Duane Reed. Rather, it's time to take a break.

There is something called a balance between being and doing. You'll need to create a balance to become still with yourself and to continually hear answers from within. Instead of running around 24/7, you'll still be focused completely on the job search, but you'll need to check in and ask yourself if you're on the right track. Are you spending energy applying to jobs that require two years of experience, which you clearly don't have yet? Or are you focusing only on jobs and connecting with people who can help you get to the next step?

Ask yourself if you will truly be happy at the job you interviewed for. Jen notes, "Tune in and check in to make sure you're on the right path." The balance requires you to sit still and ask yourself questions to accompany all the action you're doing. A lot of people show up for the interviews and return important phone calls, but they're not seeing a lot of results because they're frazzled.

Be Patient

As you follow up and continue to pursue positions that interest you and those for which you're qualified, it's super important to detach from the outcome. Just as Vincent says to not force things, give yourself a reminder to let go. Trust that something will come along sooner or later! Sure, it may not happen in your timeframe (the job search is *so* not like texting a friend and getting a response in less than five minutes). Instead, maybe in two months you'll find the ideal job that's in the path you want to pursue. Jen reminds us, "In the right moment in time, the right opportunity will present itself to me."

Feeling overwhelmed now? Never fear. You're trying to snag a job, not create a new invention or figure out the entire rest of your life at this very moment. Simply stated, do the next indicated thing: Get that first job. If self-doubts are creeping in (totally normal, by the way) and you're wondering, "What will I do with the rest of my life?" or "How will I ever get to New York City?", well, remember that attitude is everything. Simply stated, positive thoughts will help you achieve your goals. As for negative thoughts? Not so much.

Since the job search is completely new to you, of course it may feel heavy or weighty at first as self-doubts start emerging. In fact, others may tell you it'll be tough while others may be so bold as to say, "You'll never make it in New York." All the more reason to get inspired! Remember when I initially said your job search is a big ol' party? It totally should be! I wasn't lying and I wasn't sugar-coating it, either. You are creating the roadmap for a brand-spanking-new career path and the scintillating social adventures that lie ahead. Sounds pretty darn exciting to me!

Just Breathe

Jen recommends flipping it upside down. Literally. "Wow, this is a great opportunity for me to begin a life-long skill of excellent interviewing skills! I want to be teachable, I want to be open, I want to applaud myself every time I leave an interview saying, "I did really great!"

Just think about all the amazing people you'll meet during the process. After each interview, take a moment to think about what you can do a little bit better next time. Maybe there was a stumper of a question that you weren't prepared for. Maybe you didn't feel as focused because you didn't get enough sleep. Maybe you realize that eating pasta the night before won't give you as much energy as a little jolt of espresso. Okay, I'm rambling, but you get the point: Whatever the reason, take every interview, every phone call, every single e-mail as an opportunity to improve and implement the next time without being too hard on yourself.

Stay Positive in the Face of Rejection

"Every job interview and every networking event is an opportunity! Opportunities are everywhere and possibilities are endless!" proclaims an enthusiastic Jen. When you take on that energy and enthusiasm, guess what? People will notice you. You'll truly become excited about everything that crosses your path. The more authentic you are, the more psyched others will also become about your journey, and why not invite them along to hitch a ride with you? The reverse is true, too: The more you give yourself a pity party, the more you become down and out, the more people will stray from your presence. Wanna become a Debbie Downer? Then give in to your self-doubts and start listening to all the naysayers (believe me, there will be naysayers and it may come from the unlikeliest of places, like perhaps your BFF. Can we say jealous? Not everyone has the ability to pursue their own delicious dreams!)

As long as you're positive, are consistent with your goals, and stay true to yourself, you will see results. Promise. Totally not sayin' it's instantaneous, though. The process may be longer than you would have liked (isn't it always the case?), but stick with it.

Let's say that you submit two resumes to connections or jobs every week. Over three months that's 24 resumes! You're out there! You are officially in the swirl. Your name is circulating and that's just on the resume front. That doesn't include one networking event per week, weekly talks with your mentor, follow-ups with headhunters...you get the idea.

If you're feeling the idea of not taking rejection personally and re-strategizing and reassessing, fantabulous! Here's one last parting thought before we move on to other topics. Expect the best for yourself, but remember you won't always start at the top. You have to go from Point A to B to C to arrive at Point Z. Jen reminds us there's a middle ground. Instead of having one extreme or another (how's this for size? "I want to start at the top!" or "I'll never make enough money to live in NYC"), think about the middle. When you're in your early twenties, of course, you feel the burning desire to make your mark on the world by proclaiming, "Look out New York, here I come!"

Of course, it's important to keep your enthusiasm and stick to your passion, but hold onto the idea that your career is a long path. It's about progress, not perfection. As Deepak Chopra says in his book, *The Seven Spiritual Laws of Success,* focus on your intention and then detach from the outcome. Instead of putting pressure on yourself to start at the top and completely obsess over a job interview you had, why not focus on keeping the door open for other opportunities to circulate their way to you? Things don't happen overnight, so take a deep breath.

Successful people began where they were, not where they are at this moment. Think Meg Cabot, bestselling author of more than 25 series (most notably the *Princess Diaries* series) became an international bestseller overnight? Not exactly. How about Simon Cowell, television personality, producer, music executive, and entrepreneur? Betcha didn't know he started his career in the mailroom. Yes, I said the mailroom.

What about Milton Hershey of Hershey's (are you getting the idea that I have a long-term relationship with chocolate? Ahhhh.)? Well, he dropped out of school after the fourth grade (!) and had an apprenticeship at a printing press. Apparently he let his hat fall into the machine to get fired—on purpose! Then he worked for a local candy maker and launched his own candy biz. His first effort failed, as did his second—and lo and behold, his third attempt, too! He finally took a shot at the caramel business, which was finally a success. This established him as a candy maker before he parlayed that success into chocolate. Need I continue? If you look at any success story with a wow factor there's almost always a back story that makes you go, "Hmmm."

That's a Wrap

Deep down you know for sure that you'll land a job in NYC. I know you will, too. If it doesn't happen tomorrow, will the whole world end? Not exactly. Instead of thinking it has to happen pronto, wouldn't you rather have a fab job in four months than find a mediocre one tomorrow and be stuck in it? It's not a disaster, it's not doom, you're *so* not a failure. You won't go homeless, you won't starve, and there will always be someone's couch to crash on. The world won't end, the sky certainly won't fall. You'll get through the search by remaining positive, staying true to yourself, and most of all, staying calm.

There will always be a connection with a little temp job for you to pursue. There are always new people for you to connect with in order to forge ahead. Jen reminds us, "If you're willing to just relax, there's a way to make something happen."

Takeout: Resources to Go

Web Sites

Vincent Libretti: www.vincentlibretti.com

Something Different for Women: www.somethingdifferentnyc.com

Article

Steve Jobs' Stanford Commencement Address: http://news.stanford.edu/news/2005/june15/jobs-061505.html

Book

The Seven Spiritual Laws of Success (Deepak Chopra)

CHAPTER 4

THE CAMPUS CONNECTION: INTERVIEWS AND INTERNSHIPS

A h, the campus connection. At times you'll be so entrenched in searching for a job that you may overlook one of the most effective ways to penetrate the market. Here's a hint: Simply stroll into your career office on campus. They're your *numero uno* connection to recruiters that visit your campus.

Better yet, peruse the intranet's online job boards (assuming your career office has a robust site) and schedules to see when recruiters will be interviewing students at your school. You can snag an interview or at least attend an information session to rake in valuable face time with recruiters. Plus, you can also explore internship opportunities through your career office. Each school and company may have a different process; but overall, you'll need to submit your resume whether it's a full-time opportunity or internship. Recruiters will peruse the pile and either contact you to schedule an interview or have the career office do the scheduling.

If you don't land on the coveted schedule, never fear. You can always show up to a general information session to introduce yourself to the campus recruiter. Or, perhaps there are last-minute cancellations from other students. You never know. Let your contact in the career office know that you're "on call" the day of the interview in case there's a no-show. This not only shows your flexibility, it shows interest in the eyes of the recruiter that you're serious about pursuing his or her positions.

The Back-Door Approach to Working with Campus Recruiters

First things first: As you work with campus recruiters, keep in mind that they're your advocate. Most students or even recent grads may think a campus recruiter's goal is to separate the average candidates from the stellar ones. Although this is a quintessential part of the recruiting process, they have another goal in mind. They get paid to make hires. Yes, that's right. Their job, let's not forget, is to make that congratulatory phone call proclaiming, "You're hired!"

Campus recruiters typically have quotas to fill. Granted, they're not going to fill them with less than intellectual candidates just to make the hire, but they're in it to win it: They want to see you succeed. They're on your side and they want to make their numbers. In fact, they're on everyone's side. Your goal is to distinguish yourself from the pack. This means you may need to get a little creative and be open to positions that may appear to conflict with your New York goals at first.

Overall, it's actually to your benefit to pursue opportunities with a campus rep that is *not* located in New York. Say what? Well, you're not the only person who wants to live the dream, so can you imagine how many other candidates companies' on-campus recruiting representatives will meet with who have the hope to move to NYC? This means they'll put New York City as their first choice on their top city list. Everyone will. Okay, not everyone, but a whole lot more people will put down NYC than Parsippany, New Jersey.

Are you with me? Know where I'm going with this one? Your competition is very tough. Very, very tough. If you indicate that New York is your ultimate *numero uno* choice, guess what? You're immediately tossed into a pool of, let's say, a few dozen other candidates (or a few hundred, or some other very large number).

Parsippany's sounding much better now, isn't it? Guess how many people will put down central Jersey on their top city list? By the look on your face, I know it's not quite appealing; but would you rather be interviewing in a pool of four other candidates or forty?

The case for Parsippany (or any other similar location) is that it's close to NYC. Is it directly in the city? No. Can you do the reverse commute at first? You bet. Throughout your job search you'll learn the fine art of being flexible (yes, also this means considering an apartment in Astoria or Brooklyn). This applies to your job as well. Use your discretion, but just be aware that this strategy has worked time and time again.

You can definitely mention to a recruiter that Manhattan is your primary goal because why wouldn't you want them to know your intention? If they ask why you're interested in Parsippany or whatever, just tell them you want to get your feet wet on the job and NYC may be overwhelming. There is some truth to that, after all! Start out as a big fish in a small pond and work your way into the big time.

Leverage the interview to ask questions and find out whether the job in Parsippany or wherever will grant you the ability to work with the NYC team. If you're pursuing a client services position, this strategy should most definitely be in your job search toolkit. Regardless of whether you work in the Long Island, New Jersey, or downtown office, you'll be working at the client's office anyway! This very well means that even if you did accept a job in the main office in New York, you could be at a client in Connecticut most of the time anyway! The metropolitan area is quite large, so keeping all of your options open, in particular within client service, is the way to go. You'll find that even if you do land a job in Parsippany with less competition among the candidate pool, you may be in NYC most of the time, anyway.

Keep your eye on the prize: Once you're in, you're in. I don't care how you have to get in, but you just need to get there already. You can always pursue an internal transfer once you're on board. And if that doesn't occur, well, you've already been making connections in New York because it's so much easier once you're there. You can tap into transferring internally and networking your way into the heart of the city. For now, though, your goal is to get in any way you can. This is one of them.

The Campus Interview

Have I drilled it into your head that campus recruiting is a numbers game and that you, too, can come out on top? Good, happy to hear that. Now we need to proceed to the actual art of campus recruiting itself.

I would be remiss if I didn't state the obvious, sister. Yes, you know it. Most companies, if not all of them, are looking to recruit current students. If you've already missed the boat and you're a senior and weren't selected for interviews on campus, don't sweat it. All of the other strategies in this guide will ring true and you can completely focus on them.

However, if you're still in school or perhaps at the tail end of your senior year, you'll need to heed the following words. And if you're in an MBA program or graduate school, pay attention, too. If you are a recent alum within the past few years, you may be able to interview with companies through your alma mater's career center. It truly depends on your school's policies. The advantage to interviewing as an alum is that you're ready to start working pronto, whereas students still have another semester or two to finish.

> **Note:** *Oh yeah, in the name of paying it forward and manifesting positivity, if you still have friends in school you'll want to spread the gospel: Develop a relationship with your campus career center so that you won't miss out on opportunities to interview with campus recruiters.*

Standing Out

Gotta love when employers come to campus. Everyone is all decked out in the generic interview suit and leather portfolio trying to make an impression on the campus interviewers. That's all dandy, but in order to stand out, you'll need to have a stellar resume to get selected for that interview! Here's how to do it: "Take on leadership roles in campus positions," says Brendan Molloy, the northeast director of campus recruiting at KPMG LLP. "We reach a lot of our candidates through student-led organizations such as Beta Alpha Psi, the national accounting honors fraternity. If you are in BAP, there's a pretty good chance you'll have a KPMG representative on your campus. It's a great opportunity to shake that person's hand, get their business card, and keep in touch on a going-forward basis."

As you take on leadership roles within organizations, you'll have the opportunity to shine. And you'll need all the opps you can get. For one, focus on your GPA. To stand apart from the pack (and by that I mean your campus colleagues), hit the books. "Grades are taking even more importance than they have in the past," says Brendan. "They were never unimportant, but in this day and age people are going to look for any reason to look at another candidate considering there are so many of them for employers. Communication skills have become a significant priority as well."

Meet the Recruiters; but Avoid the Spiked Punch, Puhleeze!

According to a former executive director of talent at a financial services company, putting in face time with campus recruiters is critical to getting noticed. Ever heard the expression, "Half the battle is just showing up"? Okay, so even if you haven't heard it, no worries. Prior to coming on campus to conduct interviews, countless companies will have information sessions—and they are fun programs, at that! Maybe they'll wine and dine you; maybe they'll have a barbecue. Whatever the case, it's your opportunity to network as early as your freshman year.

"Campus presence is critical," she says. In fact, her former company, a financial services powerhouse, kept records of whether a student attended a presentation and whether they spoke to a company representative. "It actually got them on the schedule!"

If you think companies take it lightly, think again. Simply stated, show up. Ask questions, work the room. It'll show the employer that you're interested in their company. Hey, you never know what can happen down the road. Even if you're not selected for the next round of interviews,

(CONTINUED)

(CONTINUED)

you'll be in their system as having attended their events and expressing interest.

Oh, and when you do show up, if there's a social outing try not to get hammered, 'k? The campus reps may be young, but they're not dumb. They'll take note if you're drinking and acting inappropriately. Wouldn't that be a shame to ace the interview, interact very well with the company, and then lose the opportunity because you acted inappropriately? Our source notes, "There's no room or excuse to get hammered at a company event." And keep this in mind: This applies to the Real World, too. After you land a job, a very easy way to lose it is to be visibly inebriated at a company function. Don't say I didn't warn ya.

If your communication skills are less than adequate, it could very well be game over. Because communication with the campus recruiter will likely be electronic—whether it's an e-mail or electronic cover letter— it's an easy way to do yourself in. Can you say spell-check? Good, I knew you could.

The Interview Process

The interviewing process may differ from company to company. KPMG conducts two rounds of interviews before extending summer internship offers. The first interview will almost always be a 30-minute meeting on campus with a partner from the nearest office or from that particular school. The second round occurs in the local office, where the candidate typically meets two or three people. In particular, close to 100 students make it to round 2 and apply for many positions.

Landing Internships

Just as with full-time, permanent jobs, each company has its own process for hiring interns. Some companies recruit juniors on campus to present them with summer internship offers prior to their senior year. The goal for the student, of course, is to do really well on the job (notice I didn't say *internship;* after all, you'll want to treat it like a real job) and land an offer of full-time employment upon graduation. Other companies have different policies in terms of recruitment on campus. Instead of offering internships on campus, they interview for specific jobs upon graduation. Since each company follows its own protocol, rest assured it's in your best interest to know their process before getting into the game.

That said, an awesome strategy to get your foot in the door for a full-time job is through an internship. Consider this: You'll get to try on the company for size and see whether you like the career path, the people, the works. In turn, the company gets to test-drive you and see whether you have what it takes before committing to a full-time offer. Sounds like a win-win situation to me. And hey, it's how Brad Witter, a reporter at *Us Weekly,* fleshed out his internship into a full-on freelance gig. It's also how countless college students snag their offers before the start of their senior year.

Your Friend, the Mentor

Some internship programs are structured so that you'll be assigned a mentor. Your mentor serves as a buddy to show you the ropes and be a point of contact. Do all internships offer such a perk? Not so much.

You should put the same effort into finding a mentor that you're putting into your job search. Even if you don't think you need one, trust me, you do. It will be helpful to have someone in your corner to call you out on stuff, give you positive reinforcement, or just offer a general pat on the back when you deserve it. The relationship can be built over time (You'll give back to them as well because it's a give-and-take relationship in the same way that networking works.)

If you're wondering where to turn to find a mentor, by all means log onto social networking site "her future" (www. herfuture.com), where young women can connect with mentors across the country. Just as your job search is virtual, your mentor can be, too. Women will want to support you and help you rise to the occasion. Let them. (Your mentor

(CONTINUED)

(CONTINUED)

can totally be a guy, but on this particular site they're going to be women.)

Even though you can have a mentor in the office, sometimes it's beneficial to have one that's removed from the situation and not in your work circle. You can have more than one mentor, BTW, so why not get all the support you can?

Gabrielle Bernstein sings the praises of mentoring. The motivational speaker and author of *Add More ~ing to Your Life: A Hip Guide to Happiness* is also the founder of her future Web site. Although you can find a mentor on her site, or even through your community or through connections, the best way for the relationship to work is to seek a happy mentor. Another way to be sure it works is to set specific accountability goals and a scheduled time to speak a few times each month so that you can discuss your progress and listen to ways you can improve your job search. (And after you get a job, the nature of the conversation will naturally change to employment rather than seeking employment.)

Above all? Your mentoring relationship will work best if you fit well with a mentor who is available to help you. "Look for people who are happy, involved in an organization, available to be your mentor, and have an overall life balance," Bernstein notes.

Let's illustrate the point further, shall we? At KPMG they're focused on hiring people at least one year ahead of their start date. "More often than not we're meeting them three years out of their start date," notes Brendan.

Maximize Your Internship

Knowing that full-time offers are pretty much the result of proving yourself during an internship, how can you make the most of them? Maximize the experience.

For example, at KPMG there are about 200 interns each summer in the New York City office. "We expect a very high percentage of our interns to receive full-time offers. We're looking for them to be proactive, ask lots of questions, and not frown upon a longer commute than they were hoping for—that will go a long way in terms of their internship success."

Interning Conan-Style

Cara Weissman, an alum of Penn State, first moved to NYC during one summer of college to work for a public relations company. She won a $1,000 scholarship from her school to assist with living expenses. Cool, right? Her living conditions were to consist of a cramped 300-square-foot studio overlooking the YMCA and facing the Empire State Building. Well, lo and behold, one day before the internship began she was told that the job had been given to the niece of the company owner instead. Nice, huh?

As she bemoaned what she proclaimed to be her last meal at T.G.I. Friday's, the host overheard Cara, told her about an opening at his other job, and poof! She was brought on board at the NBC Experience Store in Rockefeller Center the following afternoon.

Sure, we know smoking is bad for you, but Cara networked it up during smoking breaks. "I used that to my advantage," she says, "polluting my lungs while forging new contacts who told me specific ways to land an internship at *Conan O'Brien*." She followed their advice and took advantage of the location of the NBC Experience Store, which was in the same building where pages, interns, and crew members of NBC shows worked.

Fast forward: Cara returned to campus at Penn State that fall only to return to NYC a few months later for the second semester of her junior year after landing "what would turn out to be an eight-month-long full-time internship of a lifetime."

(CONTINUED)

(CONTINUED)

Although it was an unpaid internship at *Conan O'Brien*, she did reap the benefits of swag in the form of free CDs and promotional merchandise for movies/TV shows, open bars, free meals for staying late, and hot dog Wednesdays. "I still have a 'guru' figurine, which played music when you pressed a button. Nothing was really practical." To help offset the cost of living in a NYC two-bedroom apartment with four roommates and a dog, she worked weekends at the NBC Experience Store.

Until she graduated from college, Cara made frequent trips to Manhattan. Whether it was getting rides from various strangers posting on ride boards or hitching along with friends who had cars, she felt there was more to be learned by spending weekends in Manhattan than waiting in line for a keg in Happy Valley. She slept on random couches of friends she made during her internship days and drank at bars that provided free popcorn/hot dogs with cheap beer to keep her full.

"It took me about three months of actually living in NYC to land my first long-term paid job as a PA [production assistant] on *Making the Band 3*."

Although Cara is currently working as a freelance casting producer, she aspires to travel to South America and return home only after she becomes fluent in Spanish. She dishes, "I believe being bilingual will help me to be a more valuable asset to companies in the future."

It all boils down to basics. If interns can follow up with assignments, meet deadlines, become engaged in the process, prove their reliability, show up where and when they're supposed to, and work well in a team as well as independently, they're putting their best foot forward and making a positive impression.

Other Ideas for Getting Internships

Before you proceed to the next step of leveraging that internship and bolstering your connections, there are other ways to get an intern gig that don't include campus recruiting. Sure, getting an internship via your campus is the most obvious one, but you can snag an internship the same way you would get a job. Whether it's via networking; job boards like CareerBuilder (www.careerbuilder.com), Monster (www.monster.com), and HotJobs (http://hotjobs.yahoo.com); association or industry Web sites like Mediabistro (www.mediabistro.com) for journalists and media folks; you can get your name out there.

You may also register on Urban Interns (www.urbaninterns.com) so that companies searching the database for interns might come across your information. This particular avenue may help get your name out there, but it's such a reactive approach. Remember, the key to your success is being proactive! As in get out there and do not sit back and take the couch potato approach. Getting on Urban Interns can't hurt you, but you can't expect to post your information and have the phone magically start ringing off the hook.

Working for Free

It pains me to say this, but let's get real. Many companies get away with providing a post-graduation internship opportunity in lieu of offering a paid entry-level position that you so rightly deserve. Your tactfulness and discretion will have to come into play here. Should you apply for short unpaid internships? Ask yourself these questions:

+ Can you swing it financially?

+ Will the contacts you make be worth their weight in gold?

+ Will you gain new skills to add to your resume?

+ Will it help you get a foot in the door for employment down the road because you've already proven yourself?

If the answers are yes, go for it; but just don't get stuck in the trap of being an intern forever.

Chris Wragge, CBS News Anchor, Saturday Host of *The Early Show*

Chris Wragge credits his internship as being the pivotal launching pad of his career. Prior to his senior year at the University of New Hampshire, Chris met with a media consulting firm that advised him to get internships, get on college radio stations, and mainly get out there. He landed an internship two nights each week at the ABC affiliate station in Manchester, New Hampshire. "It led to everything," he says. "I graduated from school and my folks told me, 'Don't bother coming home.'" In other words, they wanted him to go for the gold!

"I moved into the basement of my college roommate's parents' house and I made myself available to this station seven days a week. Finally the GM was like, 'Who is this guy? Why are we not paying him? He's going to sue us for gross labor practices!' They ended up hiring me and they allowed me to get on the air and do some college football broadcasting for them because I was a college football player."

In this particular business, Chris knew the importance of being versatile as well as being mobile. After working for a while in New Hampshire, he moved to the Hartford, Connecticut, market and then accepted a position working for Entertainment Tonight for four years. Moving on, he was employed by NBC Sports for four years and the PGA tour for four years combined, and now he has been in New York for over five years.

The keys to his success? "My work ethic. I am steadfast in my preparedness and my versatility. Versatility is everything. During my entire career path I was always a sportscaster, so sports always came easy. To be doing sports as my first job enabled me to have the ability to ad lib, to be natural, to not be afraid of the camera because I was the expert."

Chris offers the following advice sound bites:

+ **Be nice to people.** "Never take yourself too seriously and be nice to everybody because you'll see 'em on the way up, you'll see them on the way down."

+ **Mistakes are inevitable.** "You'll make your mistakes and learn how to fly. The best times you'll have in your career are when you're young, you're with other young people. They're your best memories. You're learning on the fly."

+ **Ignore the naysayers.** "No matter what happens in college and in your postgraduate years, you'll always be told, 'Go do something else, do something with less competition.' I pooh-pooh that. I say if you have a great work ethic and you want to be in this business, you can do it. It's a matter of surrounding yourself with the right people and opportunities continue to pop up. You just have to get yourself in the right position; you have to be ready to go at a moment's notice."

+ **Parting advice:** "Be prepared to work hard and make very little money. But the great thing about it is, you'll have a blast. It's the best job in the world and the further along you advance, the more money you'll make, and the easier it all becomes."

My initial inclination, however, is to advise graduates to look only for a full-time job opportunity. If you get sidetracked with a low- or non-paying internship gig, you may be thwarting your efforts and postponing your overall goal. Like I said, though, if the internship will help get your foot in the door, I recommend going for it. Because it depends on the situation, if you come across any unique internship opportunities as you're searching for your full-time job, you might want to explore them. But I would definitely make it a secondary goal—almost like an afterthought.

Coffee, Anyone?

If you do land in an internship through campus recruiting or other means, you will be so excited! After all, someone has given you the opportunity to shine. Hooray, right? Well, don't go throwing yourself a ticker-tape parade down the Canyon of Heroes just yet. Don't get an ego; check it at the door. If you feel like the low person on the totem pole, don't worry—you're right. And guess what? You won't be for long if you do it with a smile. Brendan Molloy notes, "As the intern, you're naturally going to be the one making the copies and occasionally getting coffee for the team. Interns who complain about that, maybe they're not a fit in the long run. Those that are enthusiastic about the 'small stuff' will be taking on more senior responsibility very quickly."

Want to make the most of your internship without complaining or bemoaning the fact that you're stuck at the copy machine all day? Look at your role as the opportunity to be enriched. Ask questions! Share your answers! Actually, what could be a more dashing, more delicious time in your career? You're the newbie! You don't have that many responsibilities and people won't expect too much from you, at least in the beginning. Under-promise and over-deliver. Be meticulous about your work and be open to receiving feedback. Regardless of whether your internship is in NYC, you should be open to being new on the team.

That said, if your internship is located in Manhattan, you may get a quick dose of adjusting to the fantastic city life along with a real-world job. Yes, you'll need to treat your internship as a real job. Don't let anyone tell you otherwise. KPMG offers subsidized housing in the form of various student housing organizations that provide dormitory-style living or dorms themselves. The beauty of it is that their interns can snag housing much more affordably than getting it on their own via a short-term sublet. The glitch, of course, is realizing upon graduation and working full-time in Manhattan that the subsidized housing is no longer offered—hence, sticker shock.

Janice Lieberman, Skilled Journalist, Author of *How to Shop for a Guy: A Consumer Guide to Getting a Great Buy on a Guy,* and Consumer Correspondent for NBC's *The Today Show*

Janice earned her degree in communications at Rutgers University and credits her internship at the television show *20/20* for getting her start in the industry. "That was an unbelievable internship. From there, I made contacts. I was graduating and people there knew people at WBCS-TV in New York and helped me get a job as a desk assistant." Moving on, Janice proceeded to work in Buffalo, New York, and then started working at CNBC in Fort Lee, New Jersey. Viewers can now watch her on *The Today Show.*

Regarding how to get a foot in the door, Janice says, "No one even asked me where I went to college or what I majored in. They want to know if you can write, if you can ask the right questions during an interview, if you can present yourself well. Get your foot in the door any way you can, anyone who will take you in any newsroom, magazines, paper, radio, TV, cable, Internet…say yes! Do it and do it with a smile. Do more than you have to do."

Janice acknowledges that you'll have to pay your dues. "In your first job, you're young. Work day and night. Do whatever they say plus more. It usually doesn't go unnoticed. Do your work with a smile and then say, "What else can I do for you?" I remember those interns. Just do your job; they'll notice. When you're ready and you see a position opening up, you need to ask. I would keep networking all of the time at the other places, too."

And how does she advise you to be savvy with potential employers? "You have to ask what the job entails, what are the hours, what will I be required to do. You need to know if you'll have any backup; you need to know what they'll expect of you, where you'll get any help as far as the on-air

(CONTINUED)

(CONTINUED)

> position with your look, your clothing, will they be helping
> you edit or teaching you how to write a certain way. It's a
> small industry and people jump from show to show, so once
> you're in, you're in."

Build Connections with Peers

Okay, so we established that you should not complain at the office
(complain all you want at home with no colleagues in sight; just don't
do it in the office) and that you should be open to feedback as well
as learning everything you can on this internship, treating it as a job.
Another aspect to making it sparkle is to build connections with your
peers and supervisors.

For instance, at KPMG there's a first-week orientation for interns and
their mentors (KPMG professionals who have been employed by the
firm for at least a year or two who have volunteered to serve as their
buddy for the summer). This way, the intern always has someone to turn
to, whether it's a question about appropriate attire for the office or what
to do if they have a disagreement with somebody in the office. At the
end of that orientation week, there's an event just for the mentors and
the interns. On the boat cruise there's food and socializing, and interns
are expected to make the most of it. "We make sure there's that face-to-
face introduction. If a mentor can't attend that event, they're excluded
from being a mentor because it's that important," notes Brendan.

Essentially, networking and social connections are key to your success as
an intern, and in particular as an open door to Manhattan. You'll need
these social skills on the job, so you'll most definitely need to practice
and hone them as an intern. Whether you're shaking hands with a CEO
or connecting with another intern about a study-abroad program you
participated in, be sure to leverage every invitation you get to attend
a company outing. Even if it's just eating lunch with other interns, no
opportunity is too small for you to connect with people on the team.

Reading Is Fundamental

Your internship is a chance to wow the suits. Check that, not just wow. Rather, wow in a fuchsia font with an exclamation point! Want to really go the extra mile? Do homework. If you're working on a project, why not google it to see who's an expert in the field, print it, and mention it to your boss?

Will you be viewed as a goody-goody by your peers? Who cares? Your goal is to get engaged, and that means to really throw yourself into the work. If you're at the copy machine all day long, as long as the paperwork isn't confidential (like having access to compensation details from human resources and then dishing about them at lunch is one sure way you'll get the boot), why not read it? And then do some extra research. If you're really enjoying the work, you'll know it because it won't feel like you're doing work. As you mention the topic to your boss or colleagues, the passion you have for the work will come across.

Technically, this is really good behavior training for when you start working full-time. You'll soon realize your work doesn't always end at the office, patiently perched on your desk for your arrival the next morning. Does this mean you need to be a workaholic and take work home 24/7? Nope. But, it does mean that you should accept the fact that you'll think about work outside the office and have the ability to sparkle that much brighter on the job as a result.

How to Torpedo Yourself

Now that you completely get the importance of doing well on an internship, how about ways to do yourself in? Um, how about falling sleep on the job? Doing a bad job? Total deal breakers. Brendan at KPMG says, "You have to treat it professionally at the onset and don't view it as a class you're taking. Treat it like it will be the rest of your career."

Of course, you will likely make mistakes, like showing up late to the office or not acting professionally once you're in the office. Another one is misusing technology (and by the way, all these rules apply once you're fully entrenched in the full-time gig as well). If you're on Facebook 24/7, don't be surprised when your boss calls you into her office to have a little chat. Thinking about YouTubing it during conference calls? Not prudent, sweet pea, totally not cool. Do it during lunchtime only; and even then I'd be careful. Net net: Only use the Net for work-related activities. Sure, it sounds very Big Brother, but why not use time at home to surf and time at work to um, work? Sounds like a good plan to me. Besides, who wants to be distracted by all of that? As much as you may love surfing the Net, it could be your biggest foe if you let it. Your job can be a nice little escape from all of the online stuff; being in the office and putting in face time can help you get away from the online world that so easily sucks you in.

Okay, back to reality: If your internship is in Manhattan, keep in mind that the nightlife is abundant. It's not called the city that doesn't sleep for nothing! There are always a ton of things to do, especially during summer months, ranging from free movie nights in Bryant Park to Shakespeare performances in Central Park. If you've ever snuck into college class a few minutes late, no worries, but now is not the time to arrive late to the office. Colleagues in Manhattan may be used to late nights, but they often show up to the office on time. They've already adapted to it. You haven't yet. If anything, save the partying for the weekend.

And what if your internship is not in Manhattan? Whether it's in your hometown or close to New York City, you'll still need to arrive on time. If you are in Parsippany, let's say, you still have easy access to Manhattan in all its glory. Granted, you won't be a quick subway ride away from the happenings, but you'll still have access to it. As proud as you should be of your accomplishments, you're still the little gal in the office. You still need to prove yourself. Your social life can wait for you on the weekend, at least at first.

That's a Wrap

Campus recruiting and internships are there for the taking. Just like the other approaches, put all of your coals in the fire. (Yes, even if you're an alum, you should hook up with your career office to try to take advantage of their corporate connections.)

Above all, everything you do is a stepping stone getting you closer to your dream job. You have to start somewhere and no task is too menial, too beneath you; you gotta remember that. Assuming and hoping that you impressed your boss, connected with a cool mentor, and made some new intern friends, the follow-up is key.

Flesh out those internship responsibilities and accomplishments and put them into your resume, ASAP. Seriously, incorporate them right away into your CV. Next, send thank-you notes to the recruiter as well as your boss and mentor. To get you into the LinkedIn groove train just in case you're already not riding it, most definitely connect with them on LinkedIn and ask them to write a recommendation for your profile. Strike while the iron is hot and perhaps even do it while your internship is wrapping up but has not ended.

Remember this: Your entire job search (it's a party, remember?) is your gig right now. You own it! You're the end-all and be-all, the pulse of all things good. An instigator, a protagonist, you make it all happen. Leveraging every single experience and every connection is only going to help you in the long run.

Takeout: Resources to Go

Web Sites

CareerBuilder: www.careerbuilder.com

her future: www.herfuture.com

Mediabistro: www.mediabistro.com

Monster: www.monster.com

Urban Interns: www.urbaninterns.com

Yahoo! HotJobs: http://hotjobs.yahoo.com

CHAPTER 5

DRESS TO IMPRESS: AT THE INTERVIEW, ON THE JOB, AND ON THE TOWN

The beauty of dressing for success (we'll focus on the interview suit in a sec, don't you worry) is that it doesn't cost a fortune. You can simply wear all black from the Gap or Banana Republic and stop traffic. Get a few accessories, mix and match, and poof! You're set. Wear a little makeup or do whatever makes you feel pretty. Invest in one or two really solid pairs of shoes that you can wear for comfort and style. (My personal fave? Aerosoles.)

Because your appearance is a reflection of your professional persona, it's important to play the part from head to toe. Think about it: Your work ethic, determination, organizational skills, and education are not easily seen when you first meet someone. Instead, your looks are the first things people will notice about you. That said, when you're in a meeting, you'll probably ask questions and be engaged in conversation, but what really sticks out is your appearance. Crisp and clean clothing will certainly show that you mean business and take yourself (not to mention your career) seriously. As for wrinkles in the clothes, rattled hair in a frayed bun, and long pants that severely need to be hemmed as you constantly avoid tripping on them? Not smart. Save the ratty look for the weekend, please.

Okay, now that you totally get the reason for looking put together which means the hair, the make-up, the outfit, shoes, accessories and oversized handbag (to throw your brown-bagged lunch in, of course), it's time to think like a style guru. Enter Bridgette Raes, style expert and author of *Style Rx: Dressing the Body You Have to Create the Body You Want*. Bridgette's traveled the country to share the gospel of rocking out the clothes you wear so that they don't wear you. Her advice is sprinkled throughout this chapter.

The One, the Only: The Interview Suit

When choosing what to wear on an interview, instead of taking a more generic route, think about the type of job you're interviewing for and how people there will likely dress, and then pull together a professional interviewing look that fits within the context of the environment where you'll be working.

If you're going to interview at a startup where you know the dress code is jeans for sure, guess what? You'll still need to wear a traditional suit for the interview. You can funk it up a bit with perhaps a large faux flower pin. Your outfit will express the message you're trying to convey. For example, if you're interviewing for a financial analyst position on Wall Street, you'll need to select a conservative look and accessorize with classic items like a pearl necklace, classic watch, and simple jewelry.

Dress for Success

According to Jill Pipon, a recruiter at a publishing company, you should "dress better than you think you should and act polished like you're meeting your boyfriend's parents for the first time." She says, "On the other hand, someone interviewing to be a teacher who would be working with small children would not benefit from wearing an unapproachable-looking dark suit, necessarily." Her advice? Pair it with more approachable, friendlier colors and less expensive, more practical items.

The interview is your opportunity to check out what your future colleagues are wearing and get the tone of the dress code. During the office visit, feel free to notice how people are dressed in the hallways, cubicles, and offices. Are they walking around in Banana Republic–type dresses or are they cruising the hallways wearing jeans and a casual long-sleeved Lacoste shirt? This is your chance, my friend, to take mental notes for your potential new home away from home soon. And by that I mean your new office digs.

In addition to doing your part by dressing impeccably for the interview and keeping your look minimalistic (go light on the hair products and makeup, okay?), you'll get to make a snapshot judgment. Instead of honing in on a few outlandish or conservative folks, assess the dress code situation as a whole. After all, regardless of a specific dress code, there will always be a few who prefer their Tahari suits and others who choose to dress as if they're going clubbing once the clock strikes 6.

Everyday Style

In the instance of a traditional workplace, such as a financial services company, you'll need to dress conservatively; but you still don't want to become just another well-dressed, bland, navy-wearing, shiny-shoes face in the crowd. If you don't feel the power, nobody else will—even on casual Fridays.

Above all, we are what we wear. "You want your wardrobe to speak for you," notes Bridgette, the style guru. Consider this: In the office or even at social work gatherings, there may not always be the opportunity to talk to everyone at the event, including people in high positions you aspire to grasp. "You want your clothing to represent you well and work for you in your favor." Considering that the number-one way we are perceived is based on our nonverbal communication, remember that you never have a second chance to make a first impression. This includes the basics: tidy hair, unwrinkled clothing, and shiny shoes. It shows that you pay attention to detail as you represent yourself at all times. This includes finding a tailor or dry cleaner in your neighborhood.

As you think about your work wardrobe, you'll need to think about both your job and the industry. If you work in a creative field like public relations, you may think oh yay, I can dress creatively since it goes with the job! Well, if you work for a PR department within a conservative company, you'll need to abide by the company's dress codes. Be clear on the dress code requirements at your company. Typically companies include requirements in their human resources policy handbook. For instance, if open-toed shoes are not permitted (perish the thought, right?), don't risk it. Dressing appropriately at work means that you take yourself seriously and abide by the company's rules. The last thing you'll want to do is to not be taken seriously or to be viewed less professionally just because you're wearing blue jeans instead of the permissible black denim on Fridays.

If you're feeling overwhelmed, fret not, my pretty. You don't need a ginormous closet full of tons of clothing and accessories. Think quality over quantity in a heartbeat. Quality clothing will last longer. So, unlike college clothes, which were pretty much disposable, work clothing should be seen as an investment. You'll want them to last and you'll want a wardrobe that mixes and matches with a variety of items. This way, you can do less with more. Got it?

Fashionista Math According to Bridgette Raes

"Let's say you want to purchase a basic pair of pants for $250, which seems like a lot of money, yet you figure you'll wear them at least once a week for the next year. This pair of pants only costs you $4.80 per wear. Conversely, if you buy a cheap pair of pants for $50 that wind up not lasting you more than 10 wears before they either fall apart or look worn out, these pants actually wind up costing you $5 per wear. The $250 pair of pants is the better value."

You may be the type of person who totally rocks out to the work day when you wear your corporate costume. You know what I'm talkin' about: pinstriped pants, a neatly pressed white blouse with fun ruffles, and simple Nine West black shoes. For Monday to Thursday you can't go wrong with basic looks that are interchangeable with other pieces of clothing in your closet. That means dress to impress by going with basic blacks and whites or splashes of colors.

Some people have told me they feel more productive when they dress up to work; and in New York, we never truly need a reason. Some women will wear dresses to work, which technically fall in the category of the suit. They're low maintenance in terms of not having to constantly mix-and-match (or in some cases, mis-match). Keep in mind you can never look too dressed up for work. The one day your CEO stops by your cubicle to say hello should be the day you decided to look your best instead of your worst. *Capiche?*

Casual Fridays

If you long for days on campus where you could literally roll out of bed and wear sweats to class, no problem. We're all there with ya. However, even casual Fridays don't imply you can get away with wearing your sweats in this concrete jungle. "Casual clothing is just a slightly more relaxed version of what you would wear Monday through Thursday," says our style guru. "It should always be crisp, neat, clean, and pulled together. Even if you can wear something as relaxed as a T-shirt to your job, you should have separate work T-shirts and casual T-shirts, for example."

It may be a faux pas to get completely decked out—pantyhose and all—for work on Fridays if the office gets very casual. It will benefit you more to be a joiner. It'll come across that you're a team player if you dress casually but crisply. But you don't have to lower your standards. "Just because a coworker wears casual clothing that looks as if it were picked up off the floor that morning doesn't mean you have to," she adds.

Channeling Your Inner Bond Girl on Interviews

Meet Tamsen Fadal, TV anchor and co-author of *Why Hasn't He Called?* Her book advocates becoming your "Inner Bond Girl" on dates (by being calm, confident, cool, and collected). But the same thought process applies to acing that highly sought-after job interview.

"I think appearance is critical. Not to be superficial, but if you go someplace and you're not put together—you don't have to be a size 2 and have your makeup professionally done—but if you're not put together, you're saying I don't respect myself enough to get it together and I don't have that much to offer you."

(CONTINUED)

(CONTINUED)

> This is the time to dress to impress! "You wouldn't go for a Wall Street job in flip-flops and sandals. This is saying you don't really care about the position and that you have nothing to offer the employer. Work on the outside to feel good on the inside. Her advice? "Know the job and make sure you're right for the job. If you're a sports reporter and you're interviewing at a fashion magazine just to have a job, it's probably not the right fit."

Glamming It Up After Work

So, now that you realize the importance of dressing for the interview and keeping up with the professional look well after you land a big job, I need to pause to talk about diversity. You'll need to glam it up after work! After all, your plan to become a New York City gal doesn't include working until all hours of the evening. Eventually you'll want to leave work and hit the town.

If you work in conservative industries like banking or law, the accent approach always works well. As Bridgette mentions, keep it conservative and then change your accessories after work because the base of the outfit is so simple. "Let's say someone wears a basic black suit to the office, with a basic ivory tank worn underneath it. She then accessorizes with basic jewelry and shoes like a strand of pearls, pair of diamond stud earrings, and a basic black pump." After six o'clock (we're assuming the average work day begins at 9 a.m. and ends at 6 p.m. and beyond), you can remove the basic jewelry and put on something more interesting and colorful (you can always pick up inexpensive accessories at Forever 21 at Union Square). You can also change up the shoe to something more funky and eye-catching, like a metallic sandal or quilted boot.

On the other hand, if you already work in a creative or laidback environment, Bridgette recommends the "novelty basic" strategy. Your mission, should you choose to accept: Choose basic pieces that have novelty accents or details. Instead of a plain pair of trousers, go with a pair that has a funky seam detail or novelty buttons or fabric. Instead of a basic button-down shirt, go with a shirt that has details like a funky sleeve treatment or is made from an interesting fabric. Keep in mind that you'll still need to be office appropriate, but it can be novel enough to wear after work.

Looking Good for Professional Events Outside the Office

And now we pause for a commercial break: dressing for work events outside the office! It's always important to dress the part. If your department is going out for a quarterly dinner at Le Cirque (a fancy shmancy restaurant in midtown), by all means, dress up! This doesn't mean wearing your best clubbing outfit; rather, it's a great reason to wear that Tahari suit you invested in with a pretty scarf. You'll be socializing with coworkers and sometimes even the higher-ups. What better way to make a great impression than dressing up?

Alternatively, say you have a work outing that includes a courtside lunch at the U.S. Open tennis tournament. In this case, it's wise to wear something that's corporate cool, like khakis. In other words, morph into actress mode and dress for the scene!

Wash 'n' Fold

Not sure which budget your laundry will fall into (is it groceries? Amenities? Or just in the miscellaneous category labeled "Stuff"?)? It matters not. If you want to dress for work like you mean serious business and dress for play like you're casual cool, you'll need to create time to do your laundry.

Sure, most buildings have the machines like you did in the dorms, but if you want to get fancy-schmancy, you will find a dry cleaner within a few blocks of your pad. There's regular dry cleaning, which could get expensive. And then there's the best invention ever for us city gals: wash 'n' fold.

In order to look sharp, you gotta dress sharp. And work hard. And play hard. And who has time when all is said and done? The wash 'n' fold people do, not you, silly!

(CONTINUED)

(CONTINUED)

> Here's the drill: You simply bring your laundry as if you were bringing it to your basement. Instead, people do it for you and you pay them and then pick up the satchel in a few days (or if you're lucky, here's a concept: takeout! They'll deliver it to your doorman). That's it. Pretty simple, huh?

That's a Wrap

In today's tough economic climate, it's not enough to shine in an interview. You wanted to rock out your interview suit to look poised and polished; but the look and confidence you radiate don't have to end just because you no longer need to meet with prospective employers.

Once you're on the ground and up and running in your new job, you'll need to work hard and become a valued performer on the team to keep your job. This is a given, but looking the part plays a huge role in succeeding.

You'll never get a second chance to make a first impression. Easy enough to remember, right? Always dress appropriately for your job once you're employed by taking cues from your peers and adhering to the dress code. Avoid wrinkled clothing or the hair-in-the-bun look just because you didn't feel like washing it that day. If anything, you might as well be too dressy or too polished rather than too frumpy looking, right?

Takeout: Resources to Go

Web Site

Bridgette Raes Style Group: www.bridgetteraes.com

Books

Style Rx: Dressing the Body You Have to Create the Body You Want (Bridgette Raes)

Why Hasn't He Called? (Matt Titus and Tamsen Fadal)

CHAPTER 6

GIGGING IT AND PAYING YOUR DUES

I f having a day job is clearly not your thing, nor is climbing the corporate ladder one chunky Steve Madden cork heel at a time, never fear. For creative and consultant types who dance to the beat of a different drum, it's time to think outside the cubicle, think bigger, and color yourself Big Apple red.

A temp job, freelance gig, or contractor's role is an alternative route to a dream job for people who want freedom and flexibility or simply don't know what their dream job is yet. You gotta get in the game somehow, so one way is to consider freelancing as a way to get your foot in the door and then kick it open. Consider this chapter the MapQuest version of avoiding highways: Sure, it gets you from point A to point B, but the ride is one of a different route.

Okay, let's 'fess up: The day job will always have its perks, like a steady paycheck, participation in a 401(k) plan and dental and medical health care, and a never-ending stream of free office supplies and toilet paper (believe me, you will inevitably run out of TP at home and will be tempted to surreptitiously sneak into the ladies' room to grab a roll or two for your crib—*so* not kidding!). But not everyone is lucky enough to land that perfect full-time gig on the first try.

A way to break into the full-time job scene is by stringing together gigs one at a time. You do the math: An employer spends thousands of dollars each year on an employee's technology needs, social security taxes, health insurance, yada yada. As a freelancer, guess what it costs the Mac Daddy out-of-pocket? Zip. Zilch. Nada! Although they're paying you a specific amount, typically all that other good stuff isn't deducted and it's a whole heck of a lot cheaper for them to add you to the vague head count as a freelancer than if you became an FTE (full-time employee).

Of course, you'll need to talk to a tax accountant regarding quarterly tax payments and all that other fun stuff, like setting aside a percentage of each check toward a retirement fund. But when it comes to making a splash in the job scene, whether you're looking to get a foot in the door to become a full-time hire or you want to bounce around from gig to gig, becoming an independent consultant may be in the career cards for you.

Breaking In

Here's the thing: What you have to do to land a sizzlin' freelance gig right out of school is similar in scope to a full-time job search. You'll need a resume (duh). You'll also need a whole lot of sass. In addition to conducting your job search like you would for a long-term thing, you may be able to find (er, create) pockets of opportunities by networking.

In fact, the networking skills you'll rely on will not differ from the ones you would use to land a full-time job. My advice? Pursue both. Unless you know for sure that gigging it is how you want to jump-start your career in Manhattan, you might as well conduct informational interviews with contacts by saying you're open to exploring all types of opportunities, including both full-time and contract opportunities.

Part-time is another story; I recommend that route if you can get multiple part-time gigs to fit your schedule. For example, if you want to be a Broadway actress, you can probably wait tables or perhaps get a flexible office job where you can take time off to go to various auditions without having the boss bat an eyelash.

Consider this example: Fashion Week occurs twice each year in Gotham. Believe me, you know when it's happening. Swarms of crowds (and by that, I mean the B&T [bridge 'n' tunnel] crowd) are all around, you'll have the occasional Paris Hilton spotting, and the shoes and handbags swirling the runways are *To. Die. For.* But I digress: Typically it's the second week in September and the first week in February. So, any fashionista knows the drill: Check out the Fashion Week job listings on

Women's Wear Daily, the end-all and be-all site for fashionables. As you apply to hand out the daily issue of *WWD* in the tents, one thing's for sure: Technically, you're in. It's not that hard to snag a short-term gig, so be sure to search craigslist, too. Keep in mind it's very short-term, so if your hours are 7 a.m. until 11 p.m. or midnight, do not cringe. Just remember that it's very short-term; you can catch up on sleep when it's done. But while you're in the midst of the swirl, you gotta work it, girl!

When you're there, put on the hat of roving reporter and smile (let's not forget the smile!): "Excuse me, who are you with?" or "Wow, you look like you go to a lot of fashion shows. How did you get started in the biz? I'd love to learn." A simple rule of any job search is remembering that everyone loves, loves, *loves* to talk about themselves.

So, to get them to open up to you and tell you how to get your game on, ask them specific questions and be cordial. Say "please" and "thank you" and send a thank-you note, always asking who they might recommend that you connect with. Next thing you know, you may be having a cup of Crumbs coffee (more on cupcakes later; they can and will be the death of your waistline if you let 'em!) together as you ask whether you may forward your resume to their hiring manager.

Manhattan is a very large island with countless opportunities, so finding a freelance gig is not going to be difficult; rocking out to it is another story! Whether it's a short-lived seasonal gig like handing out magazines at Fashion Week or running a registration desk at various conferences in Midtown, they all equate to opportunities to network and put your best foot forward. You never know who you can meet in a hallway or an elevator.

Finding Gigs Online

Back to the plan: As you're networking and creating opportunities, another strategy is to check out professional organizations' Web sites and remember that in any industry there is most likely a need for consultants. Whether they need a financial consultant, HR recruiter, or fashion merchandiser, professional organizations' Web sites should have all of the job listings for contract opps as well as full-time gigs.

Let's assume you want to pursue a career in personal training. With the click of a mouse you can easily begin your search! Here's a hint: Log onto www.associationsdirectory.org and you'll see numerous categories of professional associations. In the case of personal training as an example, simply click on the Sports and Fitness category, which will lead you to the main professional organization, IDEA Health & Fitness Association based in San Diego. Sure, you're looking for a sweet NYC gig; but hey, we're livin' in a virtual world. All you need to do is click on the Careers section of the site to see what opps are available in New York.

> **Note:** *If you've been an alert reader, you've noticed I have not once mentioned that your job will be a permanent job. Keep in mind that nothing in this world is permanent, not even the fab hair-straightening treatment you're jonesing for. Permanent jobs do not exist. Long-term jobs with potential are within your grasp, but permanent jobs are a figment of the campus career services office's imagination. Trust me.*

In a slow economy, for example, companies aren't exactly hiring recruiters to sit around and sift through resumes for a few open jobs to fill. But if you check out professional orgs like www.shrm.org, the site for the Society for Human Resource Management, you may be able to find contract recruiting gigs. Sweet!

Let's not forget temp agencies, either. Sure, Web sites are key, and the online world is where it's at. But you must, must, must focus on offline initiatives, too. Something as simple as sifting through the Yellow Pages for temp agencies and cold-calling them will do the trick just fine.

In fact, some agencies focus on a few specific niches. That's right, they find short-term gigs that lead to longer ones for specific industries. At The Hired Guns (www.thehiredguns.com), after you sign up and get their Gig Alert e-mails, it's game time in the areas of advertising and marketing, media and search, sales and business, creative, content, production, and envisioning (for example, general management, user experience, and so on).

Follow Your Passion

Allison Hemming, founder and president of The Hired Guns and author of *Work It! How to Get Ahead, Save Your Ass, and Land a Job in Any Economy!*, says being a top gun is all about listening to your inner drive. One way to conduct your gig search is to listen to your inner voice that sings to you.

Be forewarned that you may get pushback from your parents. Check that: Let's just assume you will get pushback. So, how are you gonna deflect the parental interference? Whether it's your parents and your career counselor and professors, you'll get it from all angles when people tell you that you need that perfect first job to work up the corporate ladder. Well, career progression is no longer like a ladder that you climb one rung at a time. Rather, it's more of a matrix or a lattice where you find your way in and through in whatever way you can.

Because your parents may have very well paid for your college tuition, the guilt factor will be there (you know, they'll want you to pursue medical school near your hometown, while you have your heart set on heading for Manhattan and a fashionista role). But if you're not passionate about something, you're definitely not going to be successful at it.

The first step is finding your passion and pursuing it full throttle. For instance, Allison has a big financial services client that has a planning department. The only way to snag a job in that department is to start at the bottom. Repeat after me: entry level. But hey, you gotta start somewhere, so it's time to suck it up. You'll need to start as a freelancer because there's no other way in. Once you're in, you'll be trained and groomed. Sure, you may be an entry-level event planner, but you'll move up fast.

Note: *Get over titles. Get over yourself. They're merely words.*

If you are driven (which I'm totally assuming you are) and want to prove yourself, you'll take whatever gig you're in and be sure to shine. You'll figure out ways not only to work independently as a freelancer, but also to fit into the organization. Do you connect well with colleagues?

Take direction well from supervisors? Instead of sitting back and waiting for an organization to give you these skills, you gotta be proactive. My advice? Go out and get them! Get in the game by freelancing and become an integral member of the team. Attend group birthday breakfasts and put in face time when there's a company barbecue. You won't have to go through performance-review procedures or other things like a full-time employee would, and you can take advantage of opportunities to let people know who you are every time they pop up.

Travel the Temporary Route

Hemming notes, "Careers are not linear and we understand how people move." The process itself is similar to a typical job search: When you see a cool gig, apply online, write a cover letter, submit a customized resume and details on why you would be fantastic for the job. The Hired Guns brings in the prospect (YOU!), preps you, and sends you out to work for the clients.

Gigs can last from a week, to a month, to even six months, to nine months, and can convert into full-time positions. "Try before you buy" is the mindset of many companies, so this puts them in the driver's seat to test you out before committing to extending an employment offer to you. The best mindset is to think about where this job opportunity may lead. It could result in a variety of new contacts, new networking opportunities, a full-time job, and the ability to gain new skills.

If you treat a freelance gig like a temp job, guess what? It'll be a temp job! If you go in with the mindset to be unforgettable and downright remarkable, you'll definitely make a positive impression with not only your manager but also everyone you come into contact with. Essentially, they'll figure out a way to keep you, even if it means passing you around from department to department until a full-time opportunity becomes available.

Hemming says, "When you make yourself integral to an organization and figure out what problems they have and how you can fix their pain, people will keep you. People will lay over the railroad tracks to make sure you don't leave."

Making Yourself Indispensible

So, Sherlock, how do you make yourself integral? Hard work. Simple as that. As you remind yourself you're only as good as your last gig, your work must consistently be top notch, A-list, and downright dazzling. You'll be able to do just that: Focus on the work.

Why would someone want to hire you again and again and again or recommend you to another colleague they previously worked with? Because you're good, that's why. You're punctual with deadlines. You produce stellar work. You get along well with others. Kinda like the main reason your kindergarten teacher thought you were oh-so-cute and special: You played nice in the sandbox.

Politics, Schmolitics

Now, as you get hired or assignments get extended, there are major perks about focusing on your work full stop instead of focusing on your work, political mind games, and whatnot. I'm not saying that corporations have a ton of BS (but please feel free to read between the lines here), but there may be a lot of politics, performance reviews, and cattiness in the office. Guess what? As a consultant I hereby declare you officially immune to the politics (well, for the most part). Sure, you'll need to kiss up to the right people, you'll want to hang with your new friends at the salad bar (or the Monkey Bar, for that matter), and you'll need to know when to draw the line. But you will likely not have to participate in some rah-rah annual summer meeting/outing on the boss's boss's boss's yacht in East Hampton (not, of course, unless you want to).

But you still need to be aware of how politics can impact your prospects. Using the example of a very cool HR contract recruiting gig at a cool company like Google: You get to try the company on for size and check out the corporate culture while, of course, enjoying free bagels at various staff meetings. Lo and behold, the assignment that was originally for eight weeks turns into ten...then turns into twelve...and poof! They decided they need to open an official position that you're perfectly positioned to scoot right into.

Screeeeeeeeeeeeeeeeeeeeeeeeeeeech! The hot-tamale-red Land Rover you're steering just hit a sudden speed bump in Central Park. It's my job, as your career guru goddess, to bring you back to reality ASAP. Can this happen in a perfect world? You bet. Is this a perfect world? Um, not exactly. Some internal employee may be gunning for that job as a promotion from a coordinator role. Someone else in accounting/finance may be bored out of their mind, already knows the hiring manager, and may be looking to make a lateral move internally. My point (and I do have one): Be your own advocate. Be realistic in knowing that there will be obstacles. It's your duty to be aware of them and overcome them. Net net: You have to speak up for yourself and self-promote.

Instead of simply applying online, talk to the hiring manager. Bring a file to show all of the work you've done and accolades you've gotten (this is assuming you do have accolades; and if not, then maybe gigging it is precisely for you! Do your job, do some damage, and move on—kidding). Just like any other career move you'll make, you need to speak up. Believe me, no one else will do it for you. Your job is to prove how valuable you are. Even though you think you may be "just a temp," you're not! If you think you're "just a temp," then you totally are. If, however, you think you're a diamond in the rough with the potential to shine brighter than many of their full-time employees, now you're talkin'.

You're their A-lister, their numero uno go-to gal. In other words: Fake it 'til ya make it! Come to meetings dressed to kill. Ask questions—or better yet, come up with solutions. Show them that no task is too menial for you to learn something from it. Whether it's fetching coffee or sending faxes, be inquisitive. Every job responsibility you're given is an opportunity to become empowered and learn all about it. Look at the bigger picture: Who are you sending the fax to, what will happen when they receive it, and why is it so critical and time-sensitive? This is not the time to be shy; and if you are, you gotta get over it. Ask questions and learn about your role as well as those of others and how they fit together into the team.

Brad Witter, Freelance Reporter, *Us Weekly*

Yes, I'm talkin' about that *Us Weekly*. You know you love the magazine: They dish the scoop on TomKat and all things Brangelina. And for this reporter, hanging out with Fergie is just another day in the virtual office.

Brad started freelancing while he was an intern at New York University. When he graduated amid a slumping economy, he discovered that the job market in journalism was almost nonexistent. To pursue a job in this field, freelancing was the only option. His internship definitely opened the door to his current gig. He notes, "Luckily, I didn't see it as settling for the lesser alternative to a full-time staff job—I still had the flexible schedule, which has allowed me to do some traveling and still make enough money to support myself."

For many freelancers, juggling a lot of projects, working with a variety of clients, and wearing many hats is the new normal. That said, right now Brad freelances exclusively for *Us Weekly* and has been able to expand his role. "I started out just covering events (red carpet, parties, etc.) but have now branched out into doing travel assignments and special projects. Just to explain 'special projects' a little bit...I am currently finishing up a month-and-a-half full-time stint in the office researching and co-writing a special-edition bookazine dedicated to the stars of *New Moon*."

"I think the best way to describe the perks of this specific job is that I really get to see how the other half lives, so to speak. I go to red-carpet events, get to attend the hottest parties at super-exclusive venues, get to see fashion shows; and what's great is that it's all for free!" Brad has found himself at charity dinners where people have paid upwards of $1,000 a plate. As for him? Free, free, free! He's granted VIP access to areas of concerts and clubs, backstage, and sometimes coveted front-row seats at Fashion Week. The list goes on and on. "There were times where I couldn't even afford a cab home

(CONTINUED)

(CONTINUED)

but was drinking and schmoozing with celebrities just 20 minutes earlier. And the most obvious, I've gotten to meet some of my favorite celebrities—that experience has been the most invaluable."

But his life has its downside. Brad reminds us, "Being a free-lancer is like being on call 24/7. An assignment can pop up at any time and not always with a ton of notice, which makes it difficult to make any sort of advance plans. Of course, you can always turn down an assignment; but obviously if you don't work, you don't get paid." Plus, he reminds us about the inevitable peaks and valleys: There are slow periods and busy periods. Slow times can be rough; busy periods not so much. But you may sit by the phone and wait to get an assignment that doesn't always come. "Your lifestyle is always in flux—it's feast or famine, which is why budgeting is key."

Pros and Cons of Gigging It

Convinced that there's a magical, mystical world where you can wake up and wear your pajamas all day long and work only when you see fit? Keep dreamin', darling. After all, as an independent consultant you may find yourself working harder, thinking smarter, working 'til the break of dawn, and sweating over lining up that next gig more than you ever could have imagined.

Aly Walansky, freelance blogger extraordinaire, says you will always have good months and bad months. "Don't fall into the trap of a good month letting you think it's a great time to go on vacation or buy yourself new boots. Saving for a rainy day has never been more impor-tant!"

Which, of course, brings up the social-life part of the equation. When your life is always in flux, your friends may not totally get that. They might not realize that you're always on call, whether it's diligently watching the financial markets in Asia or gallivanting to a press event like Brad or Aly. And they might not realize that it can be chaotic, hectic, and most of all, stressful even when the job seems to be completely glam on its surface. Since they're your friends for a reason, tactfully remind them every now and then that your hours are a bit different from theirs. They're only human and may give you some flack for not being around for birthday parties and other bashes. You may not get to see them as often as you would like due to the flip-flopped schedules; but hey, that comes along with the work territory.

Brad says, "And even if you are able to nab a celebrity for an interview, there are so many things that they will not be willing to talk about but I am required to ask anyway. This makes for an extremely uncomfortable situation and you can get major attitude, if not from the celeb directly, definitely from his or her publicist."

Aly Walansky, Beauty/Style Blogger

Aly took the scenic route to freelancing: After getting a job right out of school as a production editor at a publishing house and doing it for five years, she moved on to a job as a copy editor at a children's press. Lo and behold, the company downsized and laid off about half of its staff a year later. That's when she entered the freelance realm and has been doing it full-time ever since.

"I like getting a say in what I work on and when and how it's done. Being my own boss allows that and it also gives me an awesome sense of freedom and self-accomplishment at the same time." She can even do her work in the tropics. Seriously! "I've even taken my computer on vacation to tropical islands and worked from there! A con of course is that in most instances there's no guarantee of regular paychecks. You will finish your work on time or ahead of schedule and then often wait months to get paid for it."

The beauty/style blogger often goes to several events each week, so she works her computer time around it. In fact, Aly makes sure she completes specific daily and weekly "to-dos": both daily responsibilities and work toward ongoing projects.

(CONTINUED)

(CONTINUED)

"I love my job. I am working in a field I love. I get to write every day and make a comfortable living wage off of it. And I get to do it anywhere, anytime I want. I'm an excellent self-motivator—I love having many projects and getting a say in what I work on, when, and how it's done. Being my own boss allows that, and it also gives me an awesome sense of freedom and self-accomplishment at the same time."

Although you may not know when the phone will ring for the next gig, you may be logging in more hours than you even knew existed! And you may have to get really good at invoicing. At a day job you'll have that steady paycheck and semi-monthly timesheets to complete. As for cool independent contractors? You'll need to create your own invoice with the amount due, whether you're paid by the hour or by the completed project. And you'll need to follow up. And follow up. And follow up. And expect some clients may pay you within ten days; others may be within four months. For reals.

If Brad has attended a late-night party, he still has to go home, transcribe the interviews, type up a file, and send it to his magazine's editors before going to bed. In Brad's line of work, he's free during the day when most of his friends are at their offices. And he's working at night when most of his friends are free to hang out.

That said, his work experiences are definitely out of the box and downright unique. As if meeting Fergie wasn't enough, Brad got to take his little sister with him to the Borgata in Atlantic City, where they were treated to an amazing dinner and given VIP access to her concert and their own VIP table at the after-party. After interviewing Fergie, they got their picture taken together and yes, it was published in the actual magazine! Now, granted, not all freelance gigs are as glam as his. You won't always be able to score a one-on-one interview with Katie Holmes or attend a cocktail party in Joan Rivers's actual apartment, but you will be able to feel like you're living your life on your own terms if you manage it properly.

That's a Wrap

So, as I conclude this chapter before one of us has to go and download some Taylor Swift tunes (TMI? Ha!), consider this: Your megawatt Manhattan career is a matrix. It's a fluid motion from one step to the next to the next. It does not have to be a straight line up or over. It can go upwards, backwards at times, or sometimes feel like it's completely standing still. You may start freelancing and love not having a ton of direction from a "boss." Or, consider the alternative: You may absolutely detest it! If you think you might feel isolated, missing an actual commute and picking up a cup of Joe before heading into the office to dish about last night's episode of *Gossip Girl*, the freedom and self-starter mentality may not be for you.

That's okay. It's all okay. You will figure it out in due time and you can always switch it around. Freelance gigs can turn into full-time ones. Full-time ones may turn into freelancing (that, my friend, is called downsizing; but let's not go there right now). But the key is being flexible. As a freelancer or free agent or hired gun or whatever you want to call it, you gotta get out there. For example, Aly joined Mediabistro (www.mediabistro.com) and the Editorial Freelancers Association (www.the-efa.org), which help her network with other writers and editors.

To not only survive but thrive in this type of lifestyle, you gotta be a self-motivator—as in the type where your professor used to give you a syllabus for the entire semester and you would break it down into smaller chunks, working on self-imposed deadlines as well as his or hers as well. As Brad says, "You need to be the kind of person who works well independently without a ton of direction—there is an obvious lack of structure and you're very much on your own. At the same time, it is great because you're not chained to a desk from nine to five, there is so much freedom, and you never know what exciting thing will happen next."

What's Your Freelancing Personality?

Alrighty then, you may be convinced that gigging it is the path to delicious opportunities. But, alas, freelancing is not for everyone, either. Is becoming (insert your name here), Inc., in your career forecast? Take this quiz to find out!

If you downloaded a Michael Jackson song onto your iPod to reflect your thoughts on freelancing and the nonsteady paycheck, it would be

a. "Butterflies"

b. "Bad" (as in gooooood)

c. "Wanna Be Startin' Something"

Your preferred work wardrobe is

a. The corporate costume, baby! Suits and heels all the way.

b. Can't I just stay in my PJs all day?

c. Anything from Banana Republic.

Your work style regarding creating your own hours is

a. Militant. I am super-strict about my hours and productivity. An alarm clock is so for me. Yippee!

b. Loosey goosey; let's take a midday nap! Since I signed onto freelancing to have a flexible schedule, I get to create my own rules—and, of course, break 'em.

c. A balance of working hard one day and not so hard the next. Soooo hungover and glad I do not need to call in sick. After all, I began my work day yesterday at 6 a.m.!

If my career was a coloring book, I would color

a. Within the lines. Most definitely.

b. Color? I'd use freakin' fingerpaints!

c. With my Crayolas using mostly pastels with splashes of primary colors.

Answers:

Mostly *A*s: Congrats! You know for sure that a day job is for you. You like security, predictability, and stability—and hey, there's nothing wrong with that.

Mostly *B*s: Marching to the beat of your own drum, you thrive on the independence, ambiguity, and flexibility that freelancing has to offer.

Mostly *C*s: A mix between hardcore corporate and full-on flex-time, you need mostly structure with pockets of opportunities to be your own boss and own particular projects.

Takeout: Resources to Go

Web Sites

craigslist: http://craigslist.org

Editorial Freelancers Association: www.the-efa.org

International Directory of Professional Associations: www.associationsdirectory.org

Mediabistro: www.mediabistro.com

Society for Human Resource Management: www.shrm.org

The Hired Guns: www.thehiredguns.com

Women's Wear Daily: www.wwd.com

Book

Work It! How to Get Ahead, Save Your Ass, and Land a Job in Any Economy! (Allison Hemming)

CHAPTER 7

ACE THE INTERVIEW AND SNAG THE JOB

C onsidering all of the prep work you've done, all of the pounding the pavement time has been time well spent. You're making progress, that's for sure, even though the only true tangible result of a job search is that first paycheck.

Anyway, your downright dazzling positive attitude and copious connections have served you well. Now you enter the next phase of the party: the interview. Think of all the other stuff you've done as the appetizers, the prep work for the "big day," and you'll be good to go.

Interviews come in all shapes and sizes. In this chapter I give you all the info you need to ace any of them.

Phone Interviews Are Your Friends

If you're interviewing from a distance, your interview may initially be conducted on the phone. Lucky for you, you're an ace at phone interviews! And hey, if you're not, fake it 'til ya make it. You've conducted informational interviews already, so you're no beginner. The difference, of course, is that you're specifically interviewing for a position. Well, just 'cuz it's on the phone doesn't mean it lacks importance or seriousness.

Preparing for a Phone Interview

Ready to ace it, are ya? Treat it like a normal face-to-face-interview. Do not wear pajamas. I repeat: *Do not wear pajamas.* Even though it's on the phone, come on, take yourself seriously. You don't need to be all decked out in an interview suit, pantyhose and all, but please feel confident and put together. Oh yeah, brush your teeth, comb your hair, and be presentable. While you're at it, definitely wake up with at least 30 minutes to spare before the interview. I can't tell you how many times I've conducted phone interviews with people who literally just woke up. Of course, this created visions in my head about their unbrushed teeth, uncombed hair, and overall inability to focus.

Next, you'll need to find a quiet place to talk. If you're out and about, take time to sit somewhere in peace and quiet. If you're already in New York City crashing on a friend's couch, don't pick the day of your interview to go to Central Park. Outside noise is not preferred; again, try to keep it confidential. Plus, don't you want to focus intently on the interview without any distractions or interruptions?

Staying at home will be to your advantage in particular if you decide to talk on a land line instead of a cell phone. It's likely that reception will be clearer in general; and if they put you on speakerphone, I just think you'll get a crisper connection. It also reduces any risk that you'll lose the call in the middle of a sentence. "Can you hear me now?" is not what you want to be asking during an interview.

Shining During the Phone Interview

As for the interview itself, pay attention to verbal cues. If you need to pause a few moments before answering a question, go right ahead and take a moment to gather your thoughts. On the phone the silence may feel exaggerated, but don't you worry about that. Just focus on what you're going to say.

As for the listening part, in particular, if there's more than one interviewer on the other end of the phone it may be somewhat challenging to time your answers. Try not to interrupt them and be patient. Although you won't have body-language cues to read as they're speaking, you'll get the idea as to when to interject your answers.

Oh yeah, the main advantage to a phoner is having access to your questions and resume right at your fingertips. Heck, you may even want to pull up the company's Web site so that it's on your computer screen right in front of you. You don't have to feel badly about peeking at your questions to ask them at the end of the interview (not that you ever have to feel wrong about reviewing your questions, but some people get awkward doing this). You can easily look at the notes you previously jotted down, which illustrate examples of why you're perfect for the job.

Regarding the pretty stuff? Smile as you talk! You'll be surprised as to how much more pleasant you'll sound. As you're smiling, why not multitask and stand up! You'll be able to project your voice more and sound more confident if you're standing as opposed to sitting down. Celebrities do this all of the time on radio interviews, so why not channel your inner rock star?

Closing on a Good Note

Lastly, as you close the interview, you'll treat it just as you would handle an office interview. Ask them about next steps, when you should follow up, and where they are in the process. Then say your cordial good-byes. Hang up that phone and immediately send a thank-you note. Easy, right?

Acing the Lunch Interview

Another variation of the phone interview or office interview (next up on our "how to ace" list) is the lunch interview. This one could get a little weird, mainly because you'll shine in a less formal setting than the office. It could be scheduled a variety of ways. For starters, if the company you're connecting with has an office in your home location, perhaps you can meet with a few members of the team based in your 'hood. In turn, they can provide feedback to the New York office. If you're given the green light, they will likely fly you there for an office interview.

Another scenario is having the lunch interview in New York itself. Assuming that they're not paying travel expenses for an entry-level position, you're probably already in New York looking for your job or gigging it while looking for your job. Regardless, you snagged the meal ticket, so by all means, go on the interview.

Typically this type of get-to-know-you powwow is held with the higher-ups in lieu of a formal interview; but at other times it's held in addition to the office interview as the last round. It may be conducted with a few people you already met to solidify their decision, whereas in other instances it may be held with new people altogether. Regardless of the situation, it's all good. The employer wants to get to know you better. Are you feeling their love yet? Good, because you should.

The Basics

We'll start with the basics that are always worth repeating:

+ **Be on your best behavior.** No cursing, no talking with food in your mouth (we know how lovely that can be; refrain, please), no ordering alcohol, and no chatting on your cell phone while the food is being served (believe me, I've seen it all—not a smart move).

+ **Don't arrive hungry.** Eat something ahead of time, like a piece of fruit. Realize that you're not there to eat, but rather to fraternize. As you glance at the menu, be smart about it, 'k? Opt for the easy-to-eat salad and avoid the linguini.

What They're Looking For

Depending on the position you're interviewing for, the lunch interview could be critical to determining whether you get a job offer. Let's assume you're jonesing for a sales position where a huge part of the job involves wining and dining clients. The interviewer will specifically want to see whether you have the social skills to pull it off. Can you make small talk easily and are you well-versed on current events? How's your presentation? Meaning, are you dressed sharply and ready to get your game on, or are you a bit sloppy (which, of course, translates to not taking yourself seriously enough).

You may start becoming comfortable with your interviewer—maybe too comfortable at times. In fact, it may not even feel like you're on an interview at all, especially if you go out with a team that has a fantastic energy about them. Rest assured, they're still watching you like a hawk. Be yourself and be comfortable in your own skin, but not too comfy. Questions of a personal nature may come up, but just keep it light and steer away from the personal stuff. For instance, some candidates feel like this is an appropriate time to let their guard down and perhaps dish about their issues with debt or returning yeast infection. Okay, not quite, but you get the point: Keep things light and keep it focused on business or general topics, not your own life.

The One and Only Office Interview

Congratulations, you're in the home stretch now! Whether your future employer skipped the lunch interview altogether or had a string of interviews leading to this one, the office interview is the moment you've been waiting for.

Tell Me About Yourself

Ah, the dreaded question. It's a loaded question, isn't it? You're probably wondering how can you talk about your accomplishments without sounding like you're bragging, right? And since it's such a broad question, where should you start?

First things first. Brag all you want. Brag, brag, brag, brag! Go for it! This is the perfect opportunity to shine and talk about your accomplishments, your accolades, and precisely what you can bring to their company that no one else can.

You've probably rehearsed the answer to this question over and over again, but you can always improve your delivery. You won't want to sound like you hit the play button and you're a robot simply spewing out information. Jazz it up! Say it with a smile and show your passion and why you're unique.

Do not start from the beginning in terms of where and when you were born. Believe me, I've been witness to it and it ain't pretty. Instead, start with the here and now. Don't exceed 60 seconds. That's just enough time to give somebody a sense of what you're doing and what sets you apart while giving them one or two interesting accomplishments.

In addition, do not use the time to talk about personal things that aren't related to the job. For instance, if you love bikram

(CONTINUED)

(CONTINUED)

yoga and have the urge to dish about it during the interview, you can only imagine how the interviewer is negatively evaluating your responses. When you talk about something that's not relevant to the job, your personal stock goes down a few points (okay, more like a lot of points).

However, if you're talking about something personal that perhaps is related to the job, it could work. Perhaps you're volunteering at your local YMCA and organizing a food drive. This could demonstrate your ability to multitask and run events which—wouldn't ya know it—coincides with the event-coordination responsibilities of the job you want.

Do Some Scouting

Although I view the interview as show time, you always need a dress rehearsal before the curtains rise, right? Do some digging. You know you want to! Before the interview you'll want to reread your notes, but prior to the big day simply surf online. Go ahead, you know you want to! Google away and check out your interviewers' backgrounds (don't you worry, they've already googled you, too).

Feel free to appropriately bring up details of their professional backgrounds at the end of the interview when you can ask them questions. For instance, ask how he or she made the jump from sales to marketing. Or ask them about a research study they conducted that was recently published. Seriously. People love talking about themselves and they will hopefully be impressed that you've done your homework.

> **Note:** *The main reason to go on as many interviews as possible is for practice, so that you're well prepared and confident, cool, and collected when it matters most. If you really want this job, show your enthusiasm and don't try to squash it during your 30 minutes of shine time.*

Getting a Clue from Your Interviewer

Yes, that's right. Your interview will be uninterrupted time. Granted, your phone will be off and you'll be in the zone. As for them? You never know. I've heard about interviewers peeking at their e-mails as candidates are mid-sentence. I've caught them picking up a call during the interview itself. As much as this is your opportunity to sell yourself, it's also their opportunity to sell their company and the position to you. If they behave badly, it might give you a clue as to whether you would really want to work with them.

Do they seem harried? Do they speak down to their assistants? Do they constantly check their e-mails as if they are literally obsessed? Are they focused on what you're saying and making eye contact? Although you may not get a good vibe from everyone you meet with, the decision is yours whether to accept the position if they offer it. I met with a prospective employer once and pulled the plug on the process because I felt the environment would have been cutthroat, catty, and not at all supportive. This is your opportunity to check out all of that. You may not get a sense during a quickie interview, but just keep your eyes and ears open.

Walking into the Interview

Anyway, back to the zone. Before entering the office, take a deep breath and remember all of the homework you did about the company and position. Feel free to intersperse answers that show you did research. You can even say, "When I looked at your company's Web site before this interview, I noticed...." Let them know you did your homework and that you mean business.

Don't Be That Gal

Mike Stahl, national manager of partnership recruitment at Deloitte Tax, emphasizes the importance of avoiding saying what you're looking to get from the company. Instead of including information in your cover letter about what you're looking to gain, show them what you can offer in terms of the skills and experiences you bring to the table. "Companies want to see what you're good at and how you can contribute to their organization."

Since it is super competitive, be sure to show your unique skills and background to distinguish you from others. "Dig into your background, even if you've been a camp counselor!" says the seasoned recruiter who has also worked with campus interviewing and experienced hires.

His other advice?

+ Don't curse! "You can turn off the recruiter pretty fast."

+ The person interviewing you is not your friend or buddy, even though they may be young.

+ Be friendly and laidback.

+ Show the interviewer you've spent time in New York, even if it was only a week or a month. "I've seen kids on campus, even from upstate New York, who were overwhelmed and didn't last."

+ Include your GPA on the resume only if it's going to help you specific to your industry.

+ "Know the industry and big competition."

Mike offers hope to aspiring New Yorkers who feel they keep running into brick walls: "Some places won't let you in, but New York is so big, there's always a place to start."

Think First, Speak Second

You'll need to express that you are the right person for the job. Come prepared with several examples of how you performed something well. If you had an internship working at a swim club's main office, don't belittle it. Perhaps you managed a group of lifeguards or juggled three phone lines simultaneously? Try to select a few key points to highlight from all of your experiences. Granted, you've already been doing this in your previous interviews, so you're already a pro at this, right? <smile>

Remember to be honest. If the interviewer asks you about a specific skill set like a programming language, don't fudge your way through it. We can spot it a mile away. Simply say something like you don't have that particular expertise but you are proficient in another program that is similar. Or simply say that you're a quick learner.

Going along the lines of honesty, being truthful regarding the weakness question is critical, too! You know it'll occur, right? "What's your biggest strength?" is typically followed by the question, "What's your biggest weakness?" Of course you'll want to flip it inside out and make your weaknesses sound like a positive. Actually, use your new career as a springboard conversation. Hey, you're super-new in the employment field, so maybe it's okay to not even know what your weaknesses are yet! You might say something like this:

I'm still discovering the environment in which I work best, so perhaps a weakness is that I'm allowing myself time to discover both my strengths and weaknesses so I can know what to further develop."

Good answer. Insert applause here. Go you!

Please don't say that you are very detail-oriented and tend to micromanage your projects. I mean, you can say it if you feel comfortable articulating it, but remember to be direct in the answer and remember that the question was about a weakness not a strength. Then again, I'm not the most organized person, so I'm not going to reveal that I'll need the cubicle police to stop by my office digs and remind me to get organized every week. Instead, aim for middle ground. How about something like this:

Sometimes I get so excited about a project that I take on too much only to realize that I've bitten off more than I could chew too late in the process.

Again, use your discretion, but always talk about your weakness in terms of something you're developing. You can follow it up by saying,

I'm learning to assess my workload by holding back and saying no to specific projects.

As the interview progresses, you may feel more at ease. Guess what? The interviewer actually wants you to feel comfortable. He or she wants you to feel at ease and wants to see you succeed. Instead of viewing them as the enemy or picturing them in their underwear (not sure who ever thought this was a good idea to share), picture them as your mentor or your future boss! You'll start to go with your gut at this point.

The Home Stretch

At this point you may feel more comfortable and by the time you meet the third interviewer you might actually say yes when they ask if you would like a cup of water. (By the way, you should totally feel comfortable from the beginning.) Anyway, this is not the point to dish about your ex-boyfriend or how you want to live in New York City because you've always envied the gals from *Sex and the City*. The interviewer is not your friend; he or she is your future colleague. Remain professional and don't let your guard down too much.

And if they do ask you about why you want to move to Manhattan, please keep the social aspect secondary. What a fab opportunity to flex your skills in being articulate! Here's yet another chance to shine. Talk passionately about the career opportunities and how if you can make it here, you can make it anywhere! You may want to demonstrate that you're goal-oriented by saying you've always dreamt about a big career in the big city and you're proud to say that you're pursuing it full throttle.

The Nuts and Bolts of Behavioral Interviews

Many interviewers may ask you behavioral-type questions, which rely on your experiences. Phenomenal interviewers will want you to demonstrate how you've been able to do something. Show, don't tell. Instead of telling them you can handle a difficult situation that will arise, they'll want you to talk about a time in which it occurred.

Be truthful. You can always pull your stories from a variety of situations. Remember the disagreement you had with another officer in an honor society on campus about how to run the fund-raiser and how you ended up delegating to a team? Or how about the time you met a deadline on the school newspaper during finals week? How's that for a time-management example? The interviewer isn't looking so much for your answers but for behaviors that demonstrate you have the ability to handle it.

And oh yeah, your stories should always be truthful. If you want to make up a story just for the sake of it, it's interview over. The truth shall set you free.

What if you're stumped? The interview comes to a screeching halt, right? The interviewer asks you perhaps a simple yet elusive question like, "What are your weaknesses?" and then you say that you are a micro-manager and too detail-oriented. Buzzzzzzzzz. Two points to note: You can definitely take a moment to think before you speak. Silence is golden. Two or three seconds might feel like two or three hours, but silence is certainly okay while you gather your thoughts before proceeding. In fact, the interviewer will appreciate the thoughtful answer instead of you spewing something just to avoid silence.

Of course, you can mention as a by the way that you think it would be cool to live in Manhattan with all of the social and cultural opportunities. But you're in the interview to sell yourself for the job, so be sure your enthusiasm for Gotham is related to the job. If the position you're interviewing for has a special connection to New York, by all means mention it. If you're aiming for a financial role, talk about how psyched you would be to work in finance in the nation's financial capital! If you're aiming to work in sales for a medical device company, talk about how covering the NYC territory would be an absolute dream! Wanna be a programs manager for a nonprofit? Dish about how you've read that the nonprofit world in New York City has a variety of opportunities in this sector.

Your Turn to Ask Questions

So we'll assume the interview is proceeding really well. The interviewer's asking you questions, you're thinking, contemplating, and of course, articulating your enthusiasm along with your ability to do the job. At the end the interviewer will likely ask if you have any questions. This is where the homework part comes into play. Personally I think this is the super-fun part! Put on your journalist hat and start turning the tables! You can totally use the same questions for a variety of roles, so it's not a daunting task by any means. Here are some ideas:

+ Find out why they love their job.

+ What do they dislike about it?

+ If they could change two things, what would they be?

+ If they could do anything differently, what would it be?

+ How do they describe the corporate culture?

+ How are promotions determined?

+ Are there specific goals/objectives to be met and how often are they reviewed?

+ Is there travel involved? If so, how often?

+ Will you have a mentor?

+ Why is the position open and how long has it been open?

This is why I absolutely love asking questions. You can come prepared and look at your "cheat sheet." That's right, I said it. Cheat sheet! Go ahead and peek at your prewritten notes in your snazzy portfolio. And oh yes, if they can write on your resume, you can go right ahead and write on your notepad! If they told you traveling will occur 30 percent of the time after the first six months, go ahead and write it down. You'll be surprised how you can tap into your notes when writing your thank-you note.

Next and final question as you ask in your oh-so-polite voice, "What is the next step?" Killer. Love this question! You have every right to know where you are in the process. After all, they may be asking you if you're interviewing elsewhere (the answer, my dear, is always YES, YES, YES! Fake it 'til ya make it!). Saying that you are interviewing elsewhere will put the move on it and let them know you are *so* in demand. They'll probably say that so and so in recruiting will get back to you soon.

It's always a good sign when they get back to you ASAP with another round of interviews or even the offer. If you don't hear from them right away, follow up within a week, and then the following week. If they're not interested, you may not hear back at all. Regardless, you should always send a thank-you note. Even if you got the vibe that the boss is going to be a nightmare based on how he interacts with others, go ahead and hit send on that thank-you note e-mail. Regardless of whether you don't want to work there, or you think you bombed the interview, or you absolutely loved the company and everyone, you'll need to send a thank-you note. E-mail is fine, by the way, and oh yeah: If you are writing to more than one person at the company, be sure to vary the content since they may forward your e-mails to members of the group or the hiring manager.

So, You Think You Bombed? Really?

Sometimes during an interview you may feel like you're floundering, faltering, sinking. Chances are you didn't bomb it, so try not to be too hard on yourself.

For a little boost, you can always write down little pick-me-uppers ahead of time. Why not include little inspirational quotes like, "The only way out is through" or "Dare to be remarkable"? Sometimes all we need is a teeny little pep talk. The beauty about these little notes is that you can read them before the interview to get in the zone. If you're in a conference room waiting for the interviewer to arrive, guess what? You can take a sneak peek at a little quote or two. And particularly when you walk out of that office, take a deep breath, and analyze the interview, you'll want to read a pick-me-upper to remind yourself that no matter what happens regarding this job opportunity, you rock.

Don't worry; things get easier and better. Promise. Each interview builds upon the next upon the next upon the next. Something I always tell my career peeps to do is debrief yourself right after the interview. Whether you're on the train, car, bus, whatever, jot down a few notes. Which questions totally stumped you? Write them down and think about how you'd answer them differently next time. Was there something that made you nervous? Did their office make you uncomfortable? Did you feel like you weren't yourself; and if so, why? It's a great time to take a few quick little notes about how you think you did and what you can improve upon.

The Totem Pole Theory

According to Tamsen Fadal, TV anchor and co-author of *Why Hasn't He Called?*, there is a totem pole theory as it relates to guys' priorities when you start dating them. Yep, there's their job, apartment, dog, financial responsibilities, and at the bottom rung? You. You're down at the bottom and haven't moved up the totem pole in terms of importance.

You can see where I'm goin' with this: Sometimes we may have to ask ourselves, "Why hasn't the employer called?" Let's rely on the totem pole theory again, shall we? "People already have a full plate," she says. "The reason they might not call you back immediately is that you're not a priority. There are a hundred other things they have going on in the day and it might not be a priority even though they really need to fill the position."

So, how do ya move up that totem pole without being that stalker girl who calls, calls, and calls again? Be assertive but not too aggressive. "There are so many ways to find your potential employer on Facebook/LinkedIn/Twitter and remind them that you're there," says Tamsen.

Essentially, it never hurts to be traditional. Send a thank-you within 24 hours and leave a friendly voice mail one week later to let them know you're still interested. That said, sometimes we have to face the truth. "There comes a point where you have to be honest with yourself and say, 'This is not happening.'" If two to three weeks pass by, that's fine; but it's important to find out when they're going to fill the position or whether perhaps they filled it internally.

In order to not be kept wondering, try to gauge their urgency at the end of the interview so that you don't put yourself through post-dating (er, interviewing) agita. Specifically ask them if it's okay to call at the end of next week regarding the position. Ask how quickly they're looking to fill it and where they are in terms of timing (are they finishing up the third round of interviews?). And most of all, find out how long the position has been open (if it has been six months, you'll know they're not urgent about filling it).

Most of all, it's a fabulous time to detach and detox. Grab a Starbucks, go for a run, chill out to some cool tunes. You'll be so glad you did. Interviews can be exhausting.

Attitude of Gratitude

Here's where the party just keeps on getting more fun! Yes, I said party, and yes I said fun! Okay, so the so-called hard part is over, right? (Notice there was no mention of salary; more on this in a bit). Take a chill pill and take a deep breath. This is merely the beginning.

It's time for the thank-you note! I've received thank-you notes on stationery; but unfortunately, in this day and age, a day or two can seem too long. I'm not saying sending a handwritten note is a bad move. A thank-you note is certainly expected. But I prefer e-mails because they're brief and do what they intend to do: Say thank you and remind the interviewer about your interest in their company and job. Within 24 hours (alright, 48 at the very most), you should send the thank-you note.

Need I remind you of the basics? Spell-check for sure and don't overlook your grammar. Take your time. Instead of rushing, be sure it succinctly states exactly what you want it to say.

Following are three sample thank-you notes.

Dear Bruce,

Thank you for taking the time to meet with me today. I enjoyed learning about the position. In particular, I was impressed by the robust mentoring program within your department.

I look forward to next steps.

All the best,

Gotham Goddess

Dear Kelley,

Thank you for taking me to lunch today. In particular I enjoyed our conversation about the training program and the ability to learn from one's peers at the quarterly meetings.

Thanks again and I look forward to next steps.

Kind regards,

Gotham Goddess

If you established a really good rapport with an interviewer, you can allude to the conversation you had while maintaining your professionalism:

Dear Polly,

Thank you for meeting with me today. This job in particular interests me very much and I look forward to next steps. Also, I enjoyed our conversation about traveling to France.

Thanks again for your time.

Kind regards,

Gotham Goddess

Although it varies based on the people you interviewed with, you may sometimes get a response to your thank-you e-mail from the interviewer saying they enjoyed meeting you as well and if you have any follow-up questions to please let them know. There's typically no need for you to respond to their response.

BTW, even if your interview was for an internal transfer within a company you already work for, you should still send a thank-you message. It's a nice gesture and no one will ever think it's weird that you sent a thank-you note after interviewing. This, my friend, is simply protocol.

The Offer Is Coming! The Offer Is Coming!

Assuming things proceeded, you might be expecting an offer. And if they haven't, you'll need to rinse and repeat, rinse and repeat; perfect your skills; learn, learn, learn; and trust that eventually you will be among other college grads with your very first offer!

Before we pop a cork on the bubbly too soon, there are certain things to know about salary and how money talks (or in some cases, walks). If you're interviewing among a group of others, such as through a campus recruiting organization, salary is typically nonnegotiable. If you're offered, let's say, a salary of $50,000 for a financial analyst position along with 50 others to work at the headquarters in Dallas, chances are there is very little wiggle room.

Ground Your Helicopter Parents

Let us pause now for a commercial break. Let's talk helicopter parents. In chapter 1 you learned about the importance of squashing their involvement and redirecting their energy toward less overt pursuits. Well, it's worth mentioning again during the offer stage. Mommies and daddies have indeed phoned employers to talk dollars and cents. As you're a full-fledged grownup, please-oh-please do not let them do it. If you claim to be one of those alums who simply didn't know your mom or dad made the dreaded phone call to the company, 'fess up. They had to get the employer's contact information somehow. There, I feel better now and simply had to get that off my chest.

Now that you know you hold the reigns to your future, including ownership about salary talks, it doesn't hurt to talk money. In fact, you should start getting comfortable dishing about it. Just be advised that companies may not always have room to budge even an inch. Let's take two scenarios, shall we?

Scenario One: Group Hires

The first is the easiest one and the path of least resistance. If you are recruited among tons of other grads for a similar position in the same office, just know that your peers will be earning just as much as you are. After they make you an offer, you may want to tactfully and professionally ask, "Is there any way to perhaps increase the amount to $55,000? I understand you may not have any leeway, but I just figured I had to ask." It's totally okay to say something like that. If they come back to you and say sorry, it's a no-go, you can either say okay, no problem or try to work out a sign-on bonus. "Do you think a salary of $50,000 and a sign-on bonus of $5,000 is possible?" Again, probably not doable. But hey, you gotta ask, right? You don't want to become a pain, but if you don't ask the question you'll know the answer is already no. By asking you merely increase your shot of getting a yes. Net net: You simply have nothing to lose by asking the question.

Scenario Two: The Individual Hire

Okeee dokee, so what if your salary isn't exactly set in stone? What if you're a one-off hire for a single position that simply needs to be filled? Know your worth. Research similar jobs on Salary.com (www.salary. com). Also realize that a company has the ability to set a salary based on what they think it should be. You may think a marketing assistant job should start at $60,000, but in reality it's more like $40,000. And if you get a job in one of the commutable suburbs, it could very well be less coin than if the job were directly in the heart of the city.

Salary may come up early in the interviewing process, but technically I'm never a big fan of that. If the recruiter asks you from the very beginning about your salary requirement, simply say, "What the market will bear based on my skill set and experiences." Enough said. Good enough, they'll think, as you get the green light to pass go. If you give them a specific number up front it could become problematic on two counts.

✦ One, you may totally undersell yourself. Perhaps the job for a marketing assistant is with a huge company that compensates its employees very well. Maybe their range is $60,000 to $65,000 and you go in there meekly asking for $40,000. Guess what? They can very well pay you the $40,000. A fair company wouldn't do that, but you never know—after all, this is NYC we're talking about and employers these days are always looking to save a dime (and in the end, their shirt).

✦ The converse is true as well. What if you go in there and tell them you want at least $60,000? If the job is paying less than that, the recruiter will instantly slam a door in your face and thank you for playing.

My advice? Keep things open and be flexible.

It's your job to razzle-dazzle 'em during the interview, and when they want to extend you an offer is when you can negotiate to your best ability. Keep in mind you're new to this. Have you negotiated in the past when you upped your curfew with your parents back in high school? You bet. This is a lot different, so rest assured some people get caught up in the money talks segment of job offers. Try not to be too hard on yourself and realize that in time you will improve your skills to become a salary superstar! For now, go with the basics.

Because You're Worth It

When salaries are determined and you get an offer letter in writing (always, always, always get it in writing!) with your start date and info on benefits and all the other stuff that makes your head hurt, be sure to ask when salaries will be reviewed and then increased. If you're starting the new gig on September 15, perhaps the company's new fiscal year is January 1.

Find out if your salary will be adjusted this coming January. And if the answer's no, find out if your salary will be prorated the next year to include the next year's salary plus a three-month bump. Also, find out what the typical salary increase is from year to year and whether you're eligible for overtime as well as an annual bonus. Granted, as a brand-spanking-new college grad, they may say you're not eligible for a bonus yet since you don't have enough skills to bring to the table. Well, they may not be exactly that blunt, but you get the message. Work hard and you, too, shall be rewarded down the road.

Negotiation Walk-through

Let the employer extend an offer to you. They may say something like this:

> *Feedback from the interviewers was all positive and we'd be happy to extend an offer to you. We'd like you to join the team at $40,000 per year.*

This is where you pause enthusiastically and say something like this:

> *I enjoyed meeting with them as well; this is great news.*

But—and this is a big but—whatever you do, please don't accept their employment offer that very instant. You'll lose all of your negotiating power and won't be able to think clearly in terms of comparing it to other offers (assuming you have the privilege of comparing one offer against another).

> **Note:** *This is where I must insert a disclaimer right now about how you handle your career is at your will, so please don't start e-mailing me about how you took my advice and it backfired, 'k? On a whole when people have paused before accepting their offer immediately, it made their offer and employment more valuable.*

There are benefits to pausing. It gives you leverage. You can ask to think about it for a day. A week. Find out when the offer expires and when you'll get it in writing. After you sleep on it, always ask for more money. If you don't ask, no one else will! (That is, unless you go through an employment agency because then they'll negotiate on your behalf.) Feel confident in your ability to ask for moolah because if you stay with the company for a while, your salary increases will be based on what you previously earned there, so why not start higher, right? How about something like this:

> *I was pleased with the offer but was hoping it could be a little higher based on the research I did in the industry and location. I was hoping for a package in the low fifties.*

This is where you can totally use your discretion. Some people go right ahead and state a number. Personally, I prefer stating a range, or what your expectations are in terms of a package, because it tells the recruiter where you're coming from. Always aim higher, naturally. When you start by saying you want your package to be in the fifties, you'll probably compromise and end up in the forties. Your negotiation ability may be tempered by the fact that you come to the table with limited experience, which is all the more reason to dazzle 'em with your passion and enthusiasm in the interview!

Yet another reason for pausing is if you have more than one offer on the table. This buys you time. Perhaps you're weighing two offers because—let's face it—when it rains, it pours! My very first job out of college happened just like that. After temping for the summer I landed one job offer in October with another one right on the heels. I weighed a variety of factors, including longevity and career path potential. Although salary is certainly important, it's not the end-all and be-all.

For instance, if you're offered a job as an executive assistant at a dental office for $50K/year but you really want to snag that graphic artist job at $45K/year, which one would you select?

Keep in mind that your first job is most certainly not your last. Instead, it's a jumping-off point for bigger and better! The higher your salary starts off, the higher you can leap! Always look out for numero uno, and under no circumstances should you feel badly about asking for more money. If they come back to you and say no, ask for a bonus. Your contact in the company will probably give you the schpeil: "We need to maintain internal equity and if you were paid more, everyone else internally would need to be skewed higher accordingly." Yada. Yada. Yada. Just be glad that you asked. Believe me, you'll be glad that you asked and got the "no" instead of regretting that you didn't ask in the first place!

You Did It!

Assuming everything went well with the job offer, negotiation, and acceptance, voilà, my pretty! You have officially landed in the Big Apple in a big-time way. You can guess what happens next. Yes, the beautiful aspect of networking ensues. This is one party that keeps going 'til the break of dawn. Now that you've landed, you'll want to inform everyone you know.

Whether you send individual e-mails to a few key people who were integral to your job search or update your status on LinkedIn and Facebook, which announces it to your entire network, let everyone know where you have landed. It's extremely important to keep your network in the loop on your whereabouts. Do you have to do it right away? No. Actually, you'll have so many other important things to take care of in terms of transitioning that you might not get to it right away. Rather, if you make it a priority to send updates within the first six months of landing your new gig, you should be good to go. After all, other people may be reaching out to you soon to network. And hey, your next gig is only a connection away.

That's a Wrap

Feeling exhausted after all these interviews, whether it was a phone interview, lunch interview, office one, or all of the above? Totally normal. Sprinkle in a ton of follow-up calls, interview some more, and of course, negotiation, and you have yourself a bona fide job search. Check that, a successful one. Hooray!

You've navigated the process and honed your elevator pitch. You nailed the interview and made incredible connections along the way. Now that you're a pro, be sure to keep the job search and interviewing skill set handy. This is only the beginning of your illustrious career in the big city. And although it's your first job in New York, it certainly won't be your last.

Most of all, I'm so psyched for you! Now, diva, the party continues as you get your Gotham on. You've landed the job; in the next chapter I'm going to help you navigate landlords, roommates, and yes indeed, mice.

Takeout: Resources to Go

Web Site

Salary.com: www.salary.com

CHAPTER 8

LANDLORDS AND ROOMMATES AND MICE, OH MY!

Trust me, they will happen to you. Ruthless landlords, multiple roommates, and mice. Yes, it's plural for a reason. As in more than one. Ick. It's totally time to dish about things gone wrong and also oh-so-right to present a realistic depiction of the good, the bad, the ugly. Most of all, how can you possibly handle real-life situations and keep your real-life stress levels separate from your work life? Read on glamazon, read on.

First things first: Let's dish about the crib. Once you determine your budget and where to live, we'll figure out how to get you there. It's the age ol' scenario: Which came first, the chicken or the egg? Should you land a shiny new job and then find an apartment? Or should you set up house and then situate yourself to go on job interviews and snag a new gig? Decisions, decisions. While the choice is ultimately a personal one, this chicka says it may be wise to land your job first and then find housing in terms of figuring out your budget, your commute, whether you'll need to get a roommate, etc. This chapter gives you the info you need to make those decisions.

Living in Manhattan—or the Alternatives

As you're gearing up for the apartment hunt, you'll be in the driver's seat, girlfriend. There are several deciding factors, but the beauty of it is weighing decisions like Manhattan or nothin'! Or perhaps the boroughs are looking appealing to you as you factor in your rent, number of roommates, apartment space, outdoor space, and commuting times and costs.

Manhattan or Bust!

Due to a lack of finances or not liking the concept of living in a confined space, not everyone ends up living in the heart of the city their first go-round in the metropolis. If you are one of the lucky ones and you are indeed able to land in Manhattan, congratulations!

Granted, you'll need to get creative and resourceful. Meaning, you'll crash in an apartment with at least one roommate, if not two. Let's do some "real-world" math, shall we? If you find a listing on craigslist for $2,100/month and have two roommates, you're only paying $700/month before you add utilities into the equation. This, my friend, is a steal. Run, do not walk, to sign on the dotted line. However, it will be a 550-square-foot one-bedroom, which really means your smarty-pants roommates have already put up a makeshift wall. The bedroom is now a tiny three-bedroom (okay, more like two beds and a sofa bed) or perhaps a one-bedroom with a loft (remember them from college dorm rooms?). Ahem, bunk beds anyone?

> **Note:** *Actually the best time to move to Manhattan is right after college because you're already used to living in squalor. Anything is pretty much an improvement from your dormitory. And hey, your cramped Gotham digs may actually feel like a step up since the bathroom will be in the apartment instead of down the hall.*

Having roommates will automatically create an intrinsic social life for ya, but the key to living with strangers, a friend of a friend, or even a close friend is establishing ground rules from the very beginning. For example, find out when the rent is due to your landlord. It'll be the first of the month, most likely. But who is responsible for sending the landlord one check? Perhaps you'll each send your checks together in one big envelope. Hmmm.

Next up: Utilities. Who is responsible for paying them? What if one roommate wants to get cable with countless channels (and hey, let's face it, you will be working or partying and rarely home to watch television). Hence, why bother paying for it? How about the Internet? Are you going to go wireless or perhaps connect through your cable provider? And do you really need a landline?

As soon as you move in, it's important to have a little powwow with your roommates about everything, ranging from rent payments to utilities to even washing dishes or eating food. If you buy cereal, is it fair game that anyone can eat it? Or will you eat items only that you have personally paid for? Yet another stumper.

Living in Manhattan is certainly a thrilling—albeit expensive—ride. As you work out the details with your roommates and crunch the numbers, at least you'll know that your commuting costs will be limited to a MetroCard or taxi fares instead of hauling it from the nearby 'burbs. This is a plus!

Not to oversimplify the process, but it's really not that hard. Finding your job is a job in itself. Landing an apartment with roommates is the icing on the cake! This is the fun part and shouldn't be viewed as a chore. After all, this is the second part of the one-two punch that means you're officially beginning your big city life.

BUT, and this is a big but (hence the caps for emphasis): What if you can't afford to live in Manhattan? What if you've started looking at a handful of apartments and <gasp!>, you certainly can't live in a dark, tiny apartment where you hit your head on the ceiling and can see Ugly Naked Guy across the alley in his apartment.

Do you toss your New York City dream out the window and hitch a cab to the nearest suburb? Um, not quite, but close. Keep this in mind: Never toss your goals away, ever. Just think about them a little bit differently. Everything you want is most definitely attainable. You'll just need to spike them a bit, that's all. Enter the boroughs!

Plan B (as in the Boroughs)

Well, when it comes to living in Manhattan and all things that glitter in Gotham, you may not be one of 'em. Not at least right away, anyway. Now, I'm not saying you won't get to New York City eventually; but come on, do you really think you can afford a walkup studio apartment at two grand a month at your entry-level salary? And if splitting it a few ways is economical and within your monetary means, are you truly ready to live in a shoebox that will likely have cockroaches and a mouse (hopefully not at the same time)? Do you realize that you'll be able to access everything Manhattan has to offer courtesy of a quick jaunt on the train or bus from a nearby location?

Remember when you were in high school and applied to several colleges and simply had a safety school? You know the one. It's the just-in-case strategy—the "just in case I don't get into my numero uno college, I know for sure they'll accept me here" plan. It is time (drum roll, please) for the big reveal. Introducing (da da DUM)...Brooklyn! Or how about the Bronx? Or dare I say it, Hoboken, New Jersey? (I'm so not a fan due to the homogeneous yuppiedom, but some people happen to love it.) There are a few key reasons why you must consider the non-Manhattan places to live as a Plan B.

I'm a hardcore city girl, believe me, but when it comes to adequate living space and prices, living in New York City does not make sense. Do I live there? Oh my gosh, yes. Do I absolutely love it? Heck, yeah. Would I have been able to swing it at the age of 22 fresh out of college? Not exactly.

That said, when I first moved to Gotham it was literally New Yawk or nothin'. *So* not kidding: I moved into a tiny 285-square-foot apartment. (Sure, the landlord said it exceeded 400 square feet, but that included closet space and the hallway. But you can't exactly take a nap in the closet now, can ya?) The apartment building itself was located on a busy thoroughfare and my apartment was on the third floor facing the street side of the building. Joy. As in cross-town bus traffic noise. Both ways. Let me put it to you this way: I could literally smell a lit cigarette someone was smoking on the sidewalk or hear their cell phone ring in the middle of the night, which frequently woke me up (yep, that's how non-soundproof and –odor-proof the windows were). The apartment was dark since it faced north and there wasn't any space for a couch. No couch!

But none of this deterred me from living in a charming neighborhood in Manhattan. Eager to get out of the suburbs of New Jersey, considering a borough was not even an option for me. I wanted the true, gritty New York experience; and hey, isn't living in a crammed space with the occasional mouse (don't get me started! The handyman in the building put traps all over my floor but we never did catch the critter) part of the NYC lifestyle? I did it for three years. See, you'll have a threshold. Either you'll start in New York City and upgrade to a bigger apartment knowing what you didn't know back then. Yes, I have a couch and live on the 14th floor now—no traffic noise whatsoever. Hooray! However, I had my first mouse spotting last night. Not happy. Sometimes you need to go through the growing pains to appreciate what you'll have down the road.

If you have nerves of steel and patience to deal with some of the so-not-fun housing conditions, congrats! You're a bona fide New Yorker and you'll learn to not put up with crap from anyone or anything. However, if you're true to your finances and situation at hand, simply take a step back to realize that the NYC lifestyle equation can be altered. That's the beauty of it. Your job, your social life, and your whole Gotham existence is what you make of it. And who says the rules can't be bent into the boroughs a bit? Bend away!

Repeat after me: "Manhattan is pricey." Crazy-expensive, in fact. Rent is higher; taxes are higher; even a slice of pizza at a mom-and-pop pizzeria costs more than it would in the 'burbs. As you start heading into second-best places like Astoria (Queens) or Cobble Hill (Brooklyn), you'll begin realizing that Manhattan is not the center of the universe (shock!). You'll also start to realize how much cheaper rent is. And how much you value your space. Hey, if you play your cards right in the nearby vicinity, you may even get a backyard! Miranda from *Sex and the City* certainly did; and you can, too.

Now, of course I'm advocating living in the scintillating land of NYC with the coveted 212 area code if you can financially swing it (like maybe you have ridiculously affluent relatives or whatnot); but for the most part, we gotta be realistic and open-minded, at least in the beginning as you cast a wide net. You will make it to New York and you will create a sparkling life here, but it doesn't mean you have to start with the corner office or the amazing apartment with skyline views. Just sayin'.

The B&T Crowd

Next up, as New Yorkers scour the tri-state area for living options ranging from smack dab in the heart of the city to craigslist rooms to rent
in the nearby commutable environs, there are countless options that
technically put you in a category other than bona fide New Yorkers.
Here in Gotham we like to call them part of the "B&T Crowd." As in,
repeat after me: "Bridge 'n' Tunnel Crowd."

Yes, that's right. We know 'em, we can spot 'em a mile away; heck I
used to be one of them! The affectionate term stands for anyone who
gets to and from Manhattan via a bridge or (you guessed it) a tunnel
(ahem, the Lincoln or Holland Tunnel). I'm talkin' Staten Island. Long
Island. Shout out to Jersey!

In addition to being so near geographically but yet so mentally far from
our beloved city, it's unfortunate that the B&T crowd is privy to the
opposite of a Manhattanite's social scene, especially on weekends. The
scoop in Gotham is as follows: Tuesday night is the new Thursday (it's
the night to see and be seen, darling), Thursday is the new fashion-
forward little black dress (Thursday nights will *always* be booked on your
calendar), and Saturday nights are most definitely reserved for B&Ters.

On a Saturday night it's not surprising for Manhattanites to jet to their
Hamptons house or ski house (depending on the season), hang out
with friends and Netflix the night away, or get together for a low-
maintenance birthday party at a local neighborhood pub. Weekday
nights are when the social scene erupts here (most commuters unfortunately are constantly looking at their watch to catch a train or leaving
an event with enough time to catch a subway to Penn Station to make
their train) and on weekends? Well, they're just for tourists and people
from the boroughs.

The Case for Brooklyn

Now I know, I know, it's NYC or bust, right? Here's some
insight (but be sure to not tell anyone, 'k?). Manhattan isn't
exactly going anywhere. If your first residency in the Big Apple
boils down to a borough, it's no biggie! It's good to have goals
in life. You will get to Manhattan sooner rather than later and

isn't it good to have aspirations? Though some people who gallivant into quaint places like Brooklyn never want to leave! It's not quite considered B&T because, let's face it, no tunnel is involved and the Brooklyn Bridge is a spectacular suspension bridge in a category all its own. Instead, Brooklyn is considered an extension of lower Manhattan, if you will.

Leah Beirne is a Brooklynite and quite honestly would prefer to keep it a secret! Here's why: "I love everything about BK. I love the trees, the brownstones, the parks, the culture, the history, the ability to leisurely walk down the street, the neighborhood feeling, the separation from Manhattan, the diversity, and the sense of calm that rushes over me once I return there. I live in Fort Greene and you really can't find a better neighborhood. It's a great option because it allows you to separate work life from everything else. I love that I don't have to brave the crowded Manhattan streets and impossible brunch waits on the weekends. BK is so laidback, so much more chill."

Okay, it's time to get back to housing as it relates to this crowd, so listen up. Bridge and Tunnel people will typically get more space than their Brooklyn or Queens counterparts, and they'll most definitely live in palace-like conditions compared to Manhattanites. They'll typically pay less money and get more space. See the inverse relationship here? Gee, that makes sense doesn't it? <sigh>

New Yorkers (as in yes, "I am a New Yorker because I live directly in the city or in Brooklyn or parts of Queens close to Midtown") will claim we live here because we can't imagine living anywhere else, even if this means feeling like a trapped sardine all of the time. Borough people (for the most part it's Staten Island, Long Island, New Jersey—even though Jersey is technically another state, it still falls into the B&T category as an extension of New York—sections of Connecticut, and Westchester County of New York), on the other hand, will claim they prefer to do "real world" math, whereby they pay less, get more for their money, and have NYC within reach when they want it. Oh yeah, they also make the claim for trees and green grass. Instead of just seeing 'em in Central Park, in the 'burbs they can see them 24/7. Fancy that!

In spite of obvious reasons why B&Ters prefer their hometown, there are drawbacks. The commute to Penn Station or Port Authority via train or bus can become a royal pain in the arse, in particular during winter months. Plus, commuting costs add up and living in the 'burbs does not a happenin' social life make.

That said, it may just be in the cards for you. Just take it from Maurizio Sorbara, an analyst, who lives in Long Island and commutes to New York City. "I would love to live in Manhattan, although I think if I did I would be broke in a year." Being in the heart of the action does cost a lot of money, as he notes, "It would be hard to refrain from going out every night and spending a ton of money." Although living in Manhattan would equate to saving money on commuting charges by the Long Island Railroad (LIRR), Maurizio sounds like he knows what he's doing. Instead of living in the moment in Manhattan, he's seizing the day at home with the 'rents by saving tons of money to purchase a home in Long Island within the next two years. "Not having to pay rent or spend money for food is a blessing," he says.

And although Manhattan has countless social options on any night of the week, smarties like Maurizio get the best of both worlds by living nearby but just not immersed in the heart of the action. He not only has access to a social life in Gotham, he also has a variety of clubs, bars, and restaurants to visit in Long Island. "If the Long Island setting is not for you, a usual one-hour train ride is all it takes to get to the best city in the world. Having this convenient access to New York City is often taken for granted. There is never a shortage of activities that can be had in NYC, and a simple train ride can change a typical night into a great night. While both Long Island and NYC offer something for everyone, the main difference is the living space."

A Is for Astoria

Convinced yet? Jessica Kreider, a special programs associate in the field of event planning, was a Brooklynite turned Queens resident, all within the matter of a few fleeting months. "I love Astoria. It has all that you need and want. It has the ambiance of everything that you are looking for. It has the old-school New York feel; it's more residential with families, but also has young professionals like myself around." Communities around Manhattan don't lack in the area of restaurants, pubs, bakeries, shops, and even spacious parks.

In Jessica's new 'hood there's Astoria Park, where people can run, walk, bike ride, whatever, and listen to free concerts in the summer. The best part, aside from being 30 minutes to Manhattan via the N and W trains, is the money saved. "The rent is much more reasonable for someone just starting out and needing more space," she says. "I love everything about it!"

House Hunting 101

Since it's my job to convince ya to keep a complete open mind regarding housing and where you could possibly live (yes, that includes Hoboken and Jersey City, much to my chagrin), we need to explore a variety of house-hunting options. There are a bunch of ways to find an apartment, whether it's in Chelsea (cool neighborhood in NYC), Cobble Hill (quaint place in Brooklyn), or Clifton (Passaic County in New Jersey).

> **Note:** *Hoboken and Jersey City seem to be NYC wannabes with their urban feel. But they lack diversity in terms of restaurants and cultural offerings, IMHO.*

First: Crash on Someone's Couch

As for the first and most obvious (not to mention cheapest): Crash on a friend's couch. That's what Jess did. After meeting a nice couple at her cousin's wedding and deciding to move to New Yawk despite comments from her hometown in Michigan where people told her she would never be able to make it ("You don't have it in you," they said), she went anyway. After packing two suitcases, she hopped on an airplane and subsequently began a new life in New York. Sure, Jessica followed up with the couple and their hospitable offer and crashed on their couch for about two months in Greenpoint, Brooklyn.

Then she discovered that a friend of the family had a place in Williamsburg, so she sublet it for three months. Jess wasn't exactly feeling the hipster Williamsburg vibe, so she scoured craigslist to find new digs, which pointed her toward Astoria in Queens. "Always look at the room," she advises. "And always go with your gut."

Thanks to the Internet, you can totally do your research. And quite frankly, if you end up in a slum apartment, guess who is partly to blame? You, my dear. When you see a listing on craigslist that's too good to be true, it most likely is. That's why it's important to visit the apartment, go with your gut as Jess says, and most importantly, check it out at night.

Safety Matters

Also, as you're checking out the potential apartment, ask yourself if you can afford to pay more money to live in a doorman building with security around the clock than it would cost to live in a non-doorman building. Personally, I prefer doormen because I feel safer and it's always helpful to have someone sign for your deliveries and packages. Others prefer non-doorman buildings because they want to feel like they can come and go without having eyes and ears watching them. Whatever floats your boat.

If it's a non-doorman building, is there an intercom and video system upon entry? Or perhaps it's a part-time doorman building where the doorman is on duty from 4 p.m. to midnight. Does your building have an elevator, or is it a walkup (meaning there is absolutely no elevator and you'll be walking up five flights at least once a day)? Granted, as you're apartment shopping you'll probably be carrying only a purse or tote bag, so please envision yourself climbing all of those stairs with grocery bags or a suitcase or a laptop.

In addition to the building's security system, it's important to take the whole picture into account. In general, do you feel safe in the neighborhood, on your new block, in your new building? Are nearby restaurants open or do they close at certain hours? For instance, during the day if you go downtown to the financial district it's all hustle and bustle. But as for the evening? Well, that's a different story. It morphs into a ghost town depending on the specific street.

Erin Weed, Founder of Girls Fight Back

According to Erin Weed, a self-defense expert, founder of Girls Fight Back, and author of *Girls Fight Back! The College Girl's Guide to Protecting Herself,* nothing says safety like empowering yourself as you shop for your New York digs. Erin became inspired and empowered to educate young women after her dear friend from college was murdered. Of course, in a city like Manhattan you'll want to be safe. But even if you live in Brooklyn, Queens, or wherever, you'll need to adhere to her housing advice full throttle:

✦ Live on a floor that's not too low and not too high. For instance, living on the ground floor is not recommended because it's too easy to break into your windows. But don't live on a floor that's too high because of fire risks (that is, living on the 30th floor of a high-rise would not be prudent: FDNY ladders only reach so far!).

✦ Definitely seek buildings with doormen for an extra layer of security.

✦ Put only your first initial/last name on your door (instead of including your whole first name).

✦ When apartment hunting, pay attention if people are propping doors open and see whether foliage is overgrown. Can you still see the entry, or is it hidden by overgrown bushes?

✦ Take a great self-defense class. There will be some instances where you can't prevent harm, so becoming your own self-protector is a gift.

✦ Trust your intuition. Arm yourself. Know that if something goes down, you can handle it.

Above all, Erin says to trust your intuition and develop a healthy relationship with it. "It's one thing to have intuition and another to trust it." P.S. She strongly recommends reading *The Gift of Fear* by Gavin De Becker.

Another way to do your homework regarding safety is to ask around. As you're conducting your informational interviews for jobs, you may want to spice it up by interspersing a convo about where to live or which neighborhood your contact prefers. Perhaps ask where they live and why they enjoy it. You'll begin to notice that Manhattanites are very loyal to their 'hoods. Each neighborhood has a distinct feel; whether you're considering a few options like the Lower East Side (LES), the Upper West Side (UWS), or Hell's Kitchen (Midtown west area), they're all different.

To Broker or Not to Broker

In addition to checking out an apartment on your own for safety reasons or following up on a lead from craigslist, you can always hire someone to help you find your apartment via various apartment listings you may not have access to. Enter the real estate agent.

Now, it's not always the smartest plan to go with one if you're strapped for cash. But hey, if time is crunched and you're okay with shelling out 1.5 percent of the first annualized rent (equating to mucho dinero), by all means go for it. When the economy hits some bumps, brokers may get paid by the landlord instead of the tenant. As such they may possibly offer you one month's free rent.

> **Note:** *Don't be put off by smarmy brokers. They're not all like that. Find one you're comfortable with.*

Brokers would always love to get your business. As you attend open houses (yes, they exist for the rental market in NYC), they'll probably ask you what you're seeking in order to find your apartment. One of the best ways to get a trustworthy broker is through networking. Then again, since you're not looking to buy new digs, but just to squat in them for a while, I wouldn't recommend spending too much of your precious time researching a broker for a rental. Instead, I'd try to decide upfront how long you'll live in the new apartment. If you absolutely must dish out the broker's fee (it's typically a chunk of change to the tune of $1,500 or more), you want to be sure up front that you'll live there at least two or three years. That amount divided by 24 or 36 months is easier to swallow than envisioning amortizing it at more than $100 per month for a year, only to move yet again.

Some brokers or even rentals without a broker may have scam written all over them. As long as you're savvy about it, you won't get taken. For instance, if a landlord wants you to wire money for the first month's rent and security deposit without even seeing the apartment to rent, um, let's just say that's a huge red flag.

"Is That the Best You Can Do?"

When you take all of this info into consideration regardless of how you found your apartment, you are in charge of closing the deal. Yes, this means you'll get to negotiate with the best of them! What a fab opportunity to use those negotiating skills. Remember diva, it's a muscle that's meant to be flexed! See if your landlord will initially lower the rent or perhaps throw in a month or two for free. One way to open the conversation is by asking, "Is that the best you can do? How about another month thrown in for good measure?" Another way to negotiate the deal is to consider switching the move-in date to two weeks prior to your original moving date without paying more in rent.

> **Note:** *Keep in mind that you'll need to reserve the elevator in your building prior to your move (you'll need to do this when you move out, as well). The last thing you'll want to do is show up with all your stuff and realize you don't have access to the freight elevator.*

Flexibility is key, just as it is for your job. Maybe the hours aren't the perkiest or perhaps the boss isn't the nicest in the world, hey, it's a job in New York and is not a life sentence. The same mentality should apply to your apartment. It's your first real apartment and most definitely not your last one. Be flexible and fluid: Maybe it's time for a roommate or two to save costs and also help squash any feelings of isolation in the big city.

The Landlord Issue

Regardless of where your humble new home is located and how you snag it, you'll need to go through protocol just like everyone else. Be prepared to complete an application and submit bank statements (yes, even for a rental). Once the paperwork is complete and you pick up the keys, keep in mind that no matter what, you'll always have a landlord. Unfortunately, unlike college, your landlord is not your dormitory's resident advisor. Let's replace that friendly campus face with a landlord, shall we? Your landlord may be cool; but he or she also may not be. The point is this: You do not own your apartment and any damage done to it can equate to money out of your pocket.

Then again, your landlord may be a total wackadoo and again, looking to scrounge money out of your H&M designer jacket pockets. Cara Weissman, television casting guru, discovered this firsthand. After living in her first New York apartment in south Williamsburg, Brooklyn, for a year, she moved to north Williamsburg. "I was there a little over two years until the landlord chainsawed our front door down...he wanted to make the apartment 'bigger' without telling us and raising the rent." Needless to say, Cara now lives in Astoria.

Not all landlords will be this zany, so keep in mind that it's in your best interest to be nice to them. Pay your rent on time, don't be delinquent, and follow the rules of the tenant contract you initially signed. If it says absolutely no subletting, that means if you decide to go on a two-week trip to India you shouldn't even think about subletting your share to a stranger. If you risk it, you may seriously be kicked to the curb upon your return.

Be nice. Like I said, pay your rent on time and fulfill your responsibilities as a tenant. This means no painting (some buildings say it's okay to paint, but you'll have to restore the original color of the walls when you move out—sounds like an annoying project to me!), no major construction (now is not the time to flex your home-improvement skills to upgrade the gross kitchen sink), no nothin'. If you have any issues like a leaky pipe or something, go see your super to get it fixed. They shouldn't charge you; after all, this is why you pay them rent in the first place.

The Ick Factor

Whether you're in Astoria or Fort Greene or the Upper East Side, there's a little-known truth about Manhattan. One given, of course, is that you'll always have a landlord. As for the other? You'll end up with a mouse.

I would be remiss if I didn't mention it in the latter part of the housing section. Yes, I've been putting off writing about it, just as you've been dreading reading about it. I hate to be the one to break it to you, but at some point (usually when summer evenings turn into brisk autumn nights) you will find a mouse in your apartment. This is a solid fact. It will happen! Do not freak out; and by all means, do not pack your bags to run home to Mommy. Take one for the team and realize it's part of the NYC experience! (How's that for making lemonade out of lemons?)

The first stage of spotting the rodent is usually denial, as you'll ask yourself in all italics and then shrug it off, *"Was that what I think it was? Nah."* Lo and behold, either you'll see it again or your roomie will spot it. And at that point you officially have my permission to freak out. Of course, it'll make you feel better mentioning it to a friend or two, but here's the thing: Be discreet. Other New Yorkers will be able to totally commiserate with you and make you feel better because hey, you and I both know they've experienced this situation, too. As for non–New Yorkers? Try to keep mum with your non-city pals, will ya? They won't be able to relate, and some may even find it amusing and down-right Carrie of you. <sigh>

Your first reaction after accepting the situation will be to prop your legs up on your couch or chair to ensure that no part of your body is touching the floor. The next step, of course, is to immediately talk to your doorman or super to have the handyman stop by and install mousetraps. The super will try to make you feel better in a warped way by assuring you that the mouse has probably moved into a neighbor's pad. Net net: They should still install traps.

I don't know which is worse though: Not capturing it or capturing it. Setting up traps may result in not capturing the critter and may easily lead you to believe it's still somewhere in your radiator or—perish the thought—the dark corners of your closet or kitchen cupboard. The alternative scenario is waking up one morning to see a deceased mouse on your floor, caught dead in its tracks in the sticky trap. Double ick.

That's a Wrap

Looking for new digs equates to getting the word out you're looking for a new pad, scouring craigslist, asking around, going with a broker, or all of the above. Be sure to know your budget. And it's worth repeating to the point where you wonder if there's an echo in here: I think it's best to land a job first so you'll know what you can afford and where you'll be able to live in terms of the commute. Case in point: Would you really want to move into an apartment in Jersey City only to land an ultra-cool job in the Bronx? That commute would be a monster.

Aside from being smart about your decisions and most of all being safe, you gotta be respectful and adult-like in terms of paying rent on time, dealing with landlords, and being cordial to roommates. Lastly, your Manhattan apartment will be tiny. This is a given. The farther you retreat from New York City, the more space you'll have at a lower price point. Granted, Hoboken, Brooklyn Heights, and Park Slope are not cheap, but they're less expensive than renting a place in Manhattan. However, if you add up commuting costs and time to commute from various locations, it may make more sense to live in Manhattan after all.

Takeout: Resources to Go

Web Sites

craigslist: www.craigslist.org

Girls Fight Back: www.girlsfightback.com

Books

Girls Fight Back! The College Girl's Guide to Protecting Herself (Erin Weed)

The Gift of Fear (Gavin De Becker)

CHAPTER 9

THE MOVE ITSELF

A h, logistics. Beautiful logistics. Instead of thinking about a move as a headache, let's look at it as a way for your metaphorical career airplane to get ready for a smooth landing directly into JFK airport. You're in the final stages now and there's no turning back! You snagged not only a job but an apartment as well (assuming you decided to become employed first and then a New Yorker second). So technically, all of the groundwork is behind you.

You found an apartment that's not cockroach-infested (at least to your knowledge), met the roommates and established ground rules, and now you're ready to set up house. Although you may have been completely focused and immersed in the process for all of the other big to-do items, guess what? You're not completely out of the woods yet. You still have phone calls to make. And then soon you will be well on your way to the fabulous life.

First Things First

Okay, if you already have roommates who already live in your apartment, the move will be a lot less stressful than if you're setting up house from scratch. If it's the former situation, they've already dealt with Con Edison in turning on the electricity and they've already had the cable guy install Time Warner Cable. You'll still need to work on a few details, like ensuring that your cell phone gets good service in your apartment (and in the NYC area, for that matter). You'll want to get a new local doctor and dentist. Yes, this is where networking comes into play yet again. The best way is through referrals, chicka!

Assuming you have roommates and the house is already set up, your role (and consequently stress levels) will be considerably diminished than it would be if you were living on your own. If you don't have any roommates, you'll have to roll up your sleeves. Before you move you'll be able to make a few calls, such as scheduling the cable guy and calling Con Ed to establish service. Since your employer likely knows that you're in the midst of moving, it shouldn't be a problem to ask for personal time so you can be home when the cable gets installed, and so on. Keep in mind you don't necessarily need to take a full day off from work; perhaps you can schedule things in four-hour increments so that you have to miss only a few hours in the morning or late afternoon.

In addition to scheduling time to be home for deliveries and setting things up, you may need to take off time during work hours for personal errands and that's totally okay. Just remember getting settled in is a one-time deal and as soon as you have the big things done and out of the way, you won't have to deal with them again until the next time you move.

One main errand you'll want to run as soon as you move is dealing with the moolah. Perhaps it's time to open a new bank account that has a branch near your office or apartment as opposed to the tiny bank from your hometown, which doesn't have an office here? First of all, you can always get money transferred from your old bank to your new one. Both banks may charge processing fees, so it's something to be aware of before you do it. But at least it's an option. Another option is to get a cashier's check. Of course, if your hometown has a bank that is prevalent in New York, why not open an account at home before your big move? This way, you'll be ready to roll when you're in the city by going to another branch of the same bank.

Top Banks in NYC

+ **Bank of America:** www.bankofamerica.com

+ **Chase:** www.chase.com

+ **Citibank:** www.citibank.com

+ **TD Bank:** www.tdbank.com

The key to a smooth move is envisioning yourself removed from the chaos. Yes, you'll sometimes feel like you have a tornado swirling around you. Will it be that intense, my pretty? Um, at times, yes it will be. I'm not gonna lie. You'll need to ensure that everything that gets moved by movers or by your rented U-Haul doesn't get damaged. If you live in a walk-up, prepare to get a good workout hoofing it up and down all those darn stairs. If you hired movers, plan to tip them some cash. In the end, prepare to treat yourself to a massage or a manicure/pedicure—or all of the above.

The actual move itself should only last a day. But as for the aftermath? That will continue for quite a while. This is where it gets tricky and where stress management comes into play. If you have a lot of stuff, let's assume you'll have at least 20 boxes, if not more! Hey, even if you don't have a lot of boxes, they won't automatically unpack themselves. You can see where I'm going with this, can't ya? Depending on your personality you'll do one of two things: You'll either stay up 'til about 3 a.m. your first night in your new apartment, running on adrenaline, as you simply can't wait to unpack everything and get settled ASAP. The alternative scenario is likely as well: You'll pass out. "These boxes will be here tomorrow," you tell yourself as you drift off.

Settling in will be easier if you already have roommates because you won't have to unpack kitchen items, towels, and all the household items or decorative stuff that make your apartment a home. On the other hand, although the stuff is already unpacked, you will have no idea where anything is located!

In addition to little things like figuring out where the cereal bowls and drinking glasses are located, add your new commute to the mix, and interacting with your new roommates (assuming they're new to you; if they're a friend or former college roomie, it'll be a bit easier). Things can get dicey. Don't say I didn't warn you!

This is where New York City rolls up its sleeves and asks ya if you're serious and if you were cut out for this. Yes, you'll reach the pivotal point. I like to call it the holy crap factor. The harsh reality starts sinking in as your inner voice gets louder and louder, asking, "What have I done?" Or worse yet, "I hate it here and want to go home!"

Rome wasn't built in a day; and as much as I loathe that pithy expression, it's true. When you were a freshman in college, were you able to navigate your way to an entirely new, delicious lifestyle within a tiny little day? Nope. Were you able to connect with super-cool friends within the first week? Nope again. Instead, wasn't the transformation like a process that took time as well as trial and error?

Patience Is a Virtue

While you may be beating your head up against a graffiti-decorated wall wishing things would happen sooner, rest assured you're in motion. Heck, you're already in New York, aren't you? And by things happening sooner, I mean fully understanding your job, figuring out if your boss is a backstabber or truly has your back, and having a robust group of amazing friends.

Having it all is unrealistic, as is being able to juggle all of the transitions simultaneously. You'll begin to feel your way through your new life as soon as you embrace the process. Let yourself be a stranger to the city. Let yourself shine and perhaps walk with a new strut in your step! Maybe go by your formal first name instead of a nickname? This is the time to start fresh. So as much as you may be frustrated with everything and realize things take time to evolve, in the end you'll look back and it'll feel like your shiny, brand-new life occurred in a New York minute.

Here's a newsflash that I wish more people knew about moving to Manhattan or even its vicinity: It's different than anything you'll ever experience. Settling in takes time. Be cognizant and enjoy the process! Enjoy getting lost when you leave the subway and not being able to figure out whether you need to head north or south. Revel in the novelty of forcing yourself to take a break from your desk for a generous 20-minute (yes, I said 20) lunch break and walk around the block only to stumble upon the movie set for the latest Jennifer Aniston flick.

Allow yourself to grow. Give it time. This chapter is short for a reason. There's a fab quote by Robert Frost that says, "Sometimes, the only way out is through." You're going to experience a rite of passage every new New Yorker endures. There is no other option than trying to embrace your new life in baby steps. Seriously, let's repeat it for emphasis: There is absolutely no other option. Thinking about going home or throwing in the towel? Wimp. You can't do that. You're not going to. I won't let you.

Give it at least a year, if not longer. You chose New York for a reason. You wanted to make a life for yourself—a big city life, remember? Don't give up that dream just because it's week four and you're not feeling all comfy yet. That's part of the fun of feeling like an outsider: You need to feel comfortable with yourself before you start to fit in. Simply embrace the independence that is known so well to New Yorkers, like going to an adorable coffee shop on your own to read "Page Six" (the celeb gossip pages) of the *New York Post*. In order to transition to your new life, you'll need to embrace the stillness to connect with your city and your new life to endure all four seasons in their glory.

What could be better than boosting the end of a bad work day by watching ice skaters during the winter at the Rockefeller Plaza rink? How about celebrating a huge accomplishment at the office by treating yourself to a glass of wine at the Four Seasons hotel in Midtown? As much as you'll want to feel settled, part of the fun of not being settled encompasses enjoying some alone time and the countless ways Manhattan will become your instant companion if you let it.

Gaining Momentum, Gaining Balance

As you become more comfortable with navigating the grid as well as settling into both your work and home lives, it's a known fact that growing pains will leak into other areas of your life. It's a pretty nice shade of charcoal gray, if you ask me. If your home life is stressful (and let's say your two roommates both have boyfriends, so now your crowded apartment seems to have four other inhabitants instead of two), it's easy to let that stress spill into your work day.

On the flip side, if you're having a fabulous day at work, it's easy for that happiness to ooze its way into your social world as you pick up flowers on the way home or meet up with a new friend for a cupcake just 'cuz. What's good at the office can be good at home; what's bad at the office can morph into being super-bad at home.

So, if you're wondering how to manage it, you gotta put some mechanisms in place as your life settles into a speed walker's pace. For starters, add sincere friends to the mix. Perhaps coming home to an understanding roommate will help you vent about issues at the office and get them off your chest so that you can release the tension and focus on watching

The Bachelor. Or perhaps you're a runner and need to go to the NYSC to run a few miles. Maybe what you need is the ability to paint or attend a lecture or go out for a night on the town once you're unpacked.

The key is finding people you can trust and finding resources to back you up—check that, finding people in New York and not from home. Sure, it's great to keep in touch with friends at home, but let's just put it out there: They're jealous of you! In fact, some people may want to see you fail. There, I said it. They'll want to see you come home only to say, "I knew you didn't have it in you." Don't let them win. I would suggest avoiding talking to certain people from home as they may want to talk you out of your "go get 'em" New York mindset. If everyone could live here, they would. Not everyone is cut out to live in Manhattan. They could very well be one of those who isn't and prefer for you to be home with a low-thrills life instead of the delicious tales you'll soon be dishing!

Even if you find one person you trust—like your college roommate, your cousin, or perhaps an initial contact you made when you were networking your way to your job—you can tap into professional assistance, too. Many employers have employee assistance programs to help with stress or dealing with stuff. This way, by tackling it head on, you're not bringing excess baggage into other areas of your life. Notice I said excess baggage. It's normal to bring normal baggage along for the ride. For instance, if your roommate situation is less than stellar and perhaps your roomie has a drug problem that is affecting her hygiene and, therefore, the kitchen and bathroom are ridiculously filthy despite the fact that you constantly clean them, the stress of this can most certainly hitch a ride onto your work life. Although you may view your office as a reprieve from a stressful situation at home, it may be hard to detach yourself at the day job from the stress and unhappiness you're experiencing in your apartment.

Whether it's a counselor or a friend, depending on the situation it's always helpful to find someone to talk to—within reason, of course. Should you dish to your boss? Um, most likely not. How about your mentor? Sure thing. Be smart about who you confide in. Better yet, try to find solutions to your problems instead of creating more problems out of problems. There, I knew you weren't a drama queen, so please don't start becoming one now. That's all.

Embrace the Unknown

Take it from Aaron: For three months after he arrived at Fashion Institute of Technology (FIT), he couldn't even leave a two-block radius to go out. Overwhelmed perhaps? Maybe. But sometimes when people move here, they feel comfortable in their zone real fast; and for him it was a two-block radius. Aaron stuck it out, though, and says that just when you want to quit, everyone else is quitting, too. However, quitting is easy. After all, anyone can do it. You can try, quit, leave. Simple as that. But what's the point in that? Why not tell yourself you have two years in which to find a way to make it work; and if you're still miserable after two years, at least you know you truly gave it a shot.

The challenge is sticking it out and finding what you're made of. People who belong in New York City are the ones who are meant to be here, who love it, and who crave it and miss it when they're gone, even if it's only for a long weekend.

Our pal Marjorie Wolfe, a PR guru from Illinois, found out that while she was trying to assimilate, her hometown friends would often snicker, "You're sooooo New York!" Sure, she was landing luncheons with top-notch fashion editors to pitch the clients she represents, which seemed very *Devil Wears Prada*–ish, but guess what? That's the nature of New York. It lends itself to glam opportunities. We simply don't try to be blatant and flaunt things like having incredible experiences at our fingertips. It may inadvertently come off that we're bragging or that we're better than non–New Yorkers, and in this case Marjorie's hometown friends. The default of simply being in New York makes delicious opportunities shine that much more brightly than if we were in the 'burbs or a smaller city. We can't help it. Don't blame us for the glam factor!

Well, in the beginning Marjorie felt a bit overwhelmed. The Midwest girl uprooted herself only to adjust to the abundance of crowds, person-alities, prices, options, events, and parades. The result? She gave herself a pep talk and acknowledged that visiting Manhattan is a lot different than living here. That said, she didn't let navigating a new job and social life let her down or rain on her St. Patty's Day parade. Instead, she embraced the new opportunities full throttle without looking back. "It's simultaneous," she says. "It freaks you out and challenges you at the same time! I'm the type of person that if I get freaked out, I like to attack it head on."

> **Note:** *BTW, the St. Patrick's Day parade is a total high school crowd. Sure, it's invigorating to watch, as is hearing bagpipers all day, but it may be one of those one-hit wonders to cross off your to-do list that very first year in Gotham.*

And attack she did. Among her notable highlights after moving to Gotham? She walked so much that she dropped 15 pounds without even trying. The result? She was featured in *Glamour*! She also recalls the mindset of just getting out of her comfort zone. "New York City isn't super friendly at first. People aren't always looking to add people to their groups," she says. Anytime she received an invitation through work or new friends, guess what? She went. After all, you can always leave!

"Force yourself to leave the house, get on the train, and go." Case in point: A while ago Marjorie was invited to a record producer's party— you know the type. As you enter the building's elevator, instead of opening up to a hallway, it opens up directly into someone's apartment. "There were a lot of hipsters. People were doing coke in the back room. To succeed and be happy, you don't have to live like that. I think we stayed for an hour [as a fly on the wall] and then went to a diner and had cheese fries or something."

Staying Tough

The scene can suck you in if you let it, so you have to manage everything. Actually, in New York you might as well micro-manage it since it can tend to manage you if you don't watch your back. If you start feeling like you're being chewed on and spit back out, guess what, Cosmo gal? You're onto something! It's gonna happen. We've all been there, done that, got over it! I actually think tough periods in Manhattan make you stronger.

Look at Marjorie's story. She recognized it and knew her options. The big city could have defeated her or she could have defeated it; she chose the latter and got right out there. "Be open-minded. The New York experience can be anything you want it to be. You can party downtown or shop in Soho, do brunch, and so on. Some people are afraid to jump off the high-dive and belly flop. The worst-case scenario is you can always move home."

This is a tough city, but it makes you tougher, stronger, and more resilient. So why not aim for the diving board and throw caution to the wind? Who cares if you belly flop? You'll become tougher and smarter by sticking yourself out right away instead of retreating. You'll learn to stick up for yourself whether it's not letting a boss walk all over you, not taking any BS from so-called friends, or questioning your landlord when he or she wants to raise the rent on you. Once you start standing tall and realize you're likely surrounded by other tough cookies as well, it raises the bar. You're surrounded by strong, powerful New Yorkers. *Just. Like. Yourself.*

You will have rough days, but they will certainly get better. Keep in mind that not everyone is cut out to live in New York and that's okay, too. That's what Staten Island is for (half-kidding)! Some people, like yours truly, simply thrive on the pace, the energy, the culture, the *joie de vivre*! Others? Not so much. You might fall into the latter category.

Looking the Part

Another drawback to living conditions or the instant resiliency you must obtain is the so-called superficiality. As a reminder, we don't have cars here but we tend to do show off the bling and the Hermes Birkin bags. Hey, we're Manhattanites, what can I say? We don't wear black 24/7, though we certainly wear it a lot.

"Look the best that you can here," advises Aaron. Ever hear the term "dress for success"? Well, in New York, you dress for city success. Everything's gotta be that much more sharp and you gotta strut down the street confidently. He adds, "You'll always be 'on.' Be conscious that someone is watching you."

As you add a little spring to your step and confidently walk the walk, you'll need to know your part. Lesson number one on how to look and act on the streets involves checking out your pace. Better yet, check out everyone else's. Everyone walks with a purpose. Similar to how we communicate, the walk should be fast, to the point, and very direct. It's a funny thing about us New Yorkers: We're always checking our watches and it always feels like we're running late en route to a scintillating place.

Tech devices aren't uncommon as most people will not make eye contact while they're on foot; they're jammin' on their iPods or checking their BlackBerries, which quite honestly is not so prudent when you're crossing the street! And this is where I must interject a few words of caution. City buses? No problem. Sure, they're big and loud, but you can see 'em coming a mile away. The main thing to be careful of is messenger bikes. So not kidding! These bicyclists weave in and out of traffic like nobody's business. The key to not getting hit by one is to always look in every direction as you're crossing the street for takeout delivery guys on bikes and the ones carrying packages. Look both ways several times and know that if they come too close to you, especially as they're not obeying traffic lights, you have every right to yell at the top of your assertive New York lungs: "Hey, what do you think you're doing? You nearly hit me!"

Buses are not scary and although messenger bikes completely are, cabs fall in the gray area in between. They'll keep you on your feet for sure; but as a pedestrian, just know when the traffic light turns red they'll actually speed up to pass through it rather than halt and wait for the next legitimate green light. Walk across that crosswalk with caution.

The same process applies to your acceleration on foot, actually. When the light is ready to turn green you'll know it because the pedestrian light will change from a Walk sign/white pedestrian to a Don't Walk sign/orange blinking light that blinks blinks blinks blinks about ten times and then abruptly stops. You'll get the hang of its rhythm. Right before the illuminated orange hand abruptly stops moving is when you'll make the split-second decision to dash across the street before the cars start motoring again.

Oh, and while you're getting the sidewalk struttin' and crosswalks under control, keep your eye on the your purse, keep it shut, and most definitely wear it close to your body. Hopefully you'll never feel paranoid or be mugged (honestly, I've always felt safe in this city—knock on wood). But you just want to be street-smart, that's all. Look focused and straight ahead. Please, for the life of you, do not gawk at the monstrous buildings; that's what tourists do and you want to earn your NYC stripes, don't you? Let the tourists be tourists while you become a transplanted Gotham girl. If you need to stop someone to ask for directions in the beginning, go for it. Chances are they had to do the same as well when they got lost in the maze of confusing streets better known as Alphabet City!

The 4-1-1 on Manhattan

Ready for a textbook lesson? Good, I knew you were. Manhattan has the Hudson River to the left, the Harlem River to the north, and the East River to the east. Our precious island is divided into sections: Downtown, Uptown and (ah yes), Midtown. Fifth Avenue pretty much divides it between east and west, but for terms new to you: Think crosstown! Midtown addresses are usually in the 50s and areas can be described as a hybrid, like Midtown West if you're talkin' about 54th and 9th or Midtown East as in 51st and 2nd. Then, of course, there are the compass aliases. If you meet up with a friend on a street corner before going to a soiree, you may be specific like "The NE corner of 38th and Park."

Guess what? The same rules apply when you're in a taxi. Simply tell the cabbie the nearest intersection (and please remember to buckle up!). Just because you're inside the vehicle doesn't mean you're any safer than when you're crossing the street avoiding getting hit by one. You'll never state the name of a street without mentioning the cross-street. It'll be 51st and 2nd and you'll typically state the street first, avenue second; so it's 51st and 2nd instead of 2nd and 51st. (FYI: streets run east–west and avenues run north–south).

Plus, when it's freezing in the middle of the winter and you're cursing the long city blocks (streets are much longer in distance than avenues), you'll appreciate this little tidbit. Addresses with even numbers are located on the south side of streets whereas odd numbers are on the north; buildings with even numbers are located on the west side of avenues and odd numbers are on the east side. For instance, if you need to go to Bank of America on 345 Park Avenue between 51st and 52nd, the little compass in your head will

(CONTINUED)

(CONTINUED)

immediately know 345 equates to the east side of the street. Feeling street-smart savvy now, are ya? Go you!

That's a Wrap

Logistically, moving to Manhattan (or the boroughs, if that's your plan) is not that difficult. Granted, technically it's like any other move. Getting settled into NYC? Well, that's a whole other story.

Be prepared to have patience—a lot of it, for that matter. Embrace the uncertainty of not fully grasping your job yet or dealing with a new commute or new roommates. It may be rough at first or bumpy every now and then just when you think you have a handle on it. But you gotta have faith. The only way out is through.

Your New York experience will keep getting better and better if you wait things out and become a stronger person in the process. Sure, your home life will overflow into your work life and vice versa, so the key is finding stress-management mechanisms and a support system to help you not only survive but thrive. You'll need to rely on these mechanisms and build upon them, so keep them handy throughout your adult life for sure.

The beauty of the transition is loving every moment: As soon as you learn to navigate and learn the ropes, you'll officially be in the honeymoon stage. The key is to keep the romance alive, never letting the honeymoon stage fade. New York is so ginormous and there's always something new to check out and cool new people are just waiting to meet you. Even the word "new" is in the city's name!

Takeout: Resources to Go

Web Sites

Con Edison: www.conedison.com

Moving Center: www.movingcenter.com

Time Warner Cable: www.timewarnercable.com

CHAPTER 10

BE A TOURIST (OR NOT)

Overheard on the 6 train:

"Excuse me, but we're from out of town. Do you know how to get to 7th and 2nd Avenue?" asks the tourist wearing all plaid with an old-fashioned camera around her neck while clutching an MTA map, meekly attempting to decipher it like she's translating a foreign language.

"Sure," says the way-too-skinny hipster with black eyeliner, a nose ring, and tattered tote bag. *"I live on Avenue B, so we'll get off at Bleecker and transfer to the V; you can follow me."*

"Great, thanks!" replies the tourist in total disbelief. This New Yorker wasn't only nice, she was helpful as well. *"How long have you lived here?"* she adds to keep the convo flowing.

"I just moved here six weeks ago. I'm going to school at Parsons."

"Oh, nice," says the tourist even though she doesn't have a clue what Parsons is (hint: it's a school of design). *"Where are you from originally?"*

"Pittsburgh." <long pause> *"Different,"* she finally says with a Cheshire-cat smile and a nod.

Different. In one little word, that Lower East Sider succinctly summed up the New York experience: Different. As in not the same. As in extraordinary. We ain't in Kansas anymore, that's for sure.

Not only is NYC different, it's also important to note that it's not everyone's home base. Most Manhattanites had a home town at some point in their lives and then they moved to NYC. Sound familiar? They had to learn the ropes just like you did. They, too, experienced the highs and lows of the city, such as feeling like a tiny little fish floundering in a big ocean. And then they experienced the transformation of feeling like they could eventually be a big fish in a small pond. It's weird because eventually they start feeling like a big fish in a small pond, whether it's belonging to various associations (houses of worship, professional organizations, sporting groups, and so on) or bumping into people they know on the street, it ends up feeling like a lot of little interconnected neighborhoods rather than a mammoth city.

Please keep this in mind and don't you ever forget it: It takes time to navigate. The first few months, after you get through some bumpy patches, you'll be in the honeymoon phase for sure. During this time it's recommended by moi that you cross all the touristy stuff off your to-do list by making it a priority. Does this mean you'll go to Rockefeller Center or zip to the top of the Empire State Building? You bet. It makes sense to marvel at some of the touristy stuff since

+ You're still new, so why not marvel all you want? and

+ You'll have some time on your hands because you're not firmly entrenched in a social circle yet.

Once you are immersed in your city-gal life, rest assured that the touristy stuff will start falling to the bottom of your priority list (as it should).

Go Ahead, Hop on That Double-Decker Bus

It took me four entire years before I finally took a Saturday to venture to Ellis Island...four years! Be sure to go sightseeing as soon as you get here; and if that means hopping on a fire-engine-red double-decker bus, by all means, do it! (I did, even if it was a tour throughout Brooklyn.

The Brooklyn loop took me three years to cross off my list.) The tourist mode looks like this:

+ Go to the Guggenheim uptown.

+ Shop at South Street Seaport downtown.

+ Most definitely see a performance of the Nutcracker at Lincoln Center your very first holiday season.

+ Travel to Queens for the U.S. Open tennis tourney at the end of your first summer.

+ Check out the Mostly Mozart concerts at Lincoln Center.

Stop me any time now…

Once you get it out of your system, you'll be so glad you did. Keep in mind, of course, that you can always go back; but chances are that once your life picks up speed, you'll have other stuff on your plate as new, quirky hidden gems of New York start emerging, like visiting the small FDNY museum downtown or perhaps checking out a Big Onion walking tour about the history of the West Village.

Entertaining Visitors from Home

Plus, there will always be out-of-town friends who want to visit you and check out the major attractions, too. (And let's face it, now that you're a Manhattanite, your personal stock literally has risen 100 points!)

You're in demand. The city is in demand. Rest assured, you will have visitors from home. Walk the Brooklyn Bridge, catch a Broadway show (also realize that when you're in Manhattan and your out-of-town friend is dying to have cheesecake in Times Square, it's not considered New York cheesecake. It's just cheesecake here. Ha!), or go to Ground Zero to pay your respects.

Yes, the sightseeing will get old and expensive, so you may want to do it only in small doses. If you don't make it a priority, though, the next thing you know you'll be here 10 years and will have yet to see a Shakespearean performance in Central Park during the summer. Your visitors will no doubt remind you of all the touristy things on their list; and as such, it will become enmeshed on yours as well. Although it's fun experiencing your beloved city through their eyes, you will *so* not marvel at the blinding neon lights of Times Square. Remind your friends that there are lesser-known parts of Gotham that are way more charming and intimate.

Note: *You will have visitors. This is another part of the process of weeding out the friends. Some friends or relatives are true and will want to see you while having a blast in your new city. Others? Not so much. They'll just be happy they have a free place to crash and then they'll want you to spend precious cash on dinner, drinks, B'way…you get the idea.*

Oh, this is a biggie. Some out-of-towners will expect you to have a car. Even though they know you don't have one because you'll remind them, of course, they'll think you'll magically pick them up at the airport and whisk them away to Gotham, luggage and all. Here's a wakeup call: Simply tell them you don't have a car and, therefore, logistically won't be able to pick them up. Give them three options:

+ **Take a cab.** Cabs typically cost about 60 bucks from nearby airports to any point in the city.

+ **Catch the train or bus.** They can take a train for the cost of a subway fare (see www.panynj.gov/airports/). For public transportation to and from JFK, simply hop on the AirTrain. Three AirTrain JFK routes stop at every terminal: The All Terminals Route, the Howard Beach Route, and the Jamaica Station Route. These particular routes can then connect you to New York City subways and buses, the most prevalent connection being the train at Jamaica Station. As for LaGuardia, simply hop on the M60 bus at the airport and you'll get dropped off at 106th and Broadway. Regarding Newark, take the free AirTrain to Airport Station to connect to NJ Transit, which will take you to Penn Station.

+ **Get a shuttle.** They can grab a shuttle for about 15 bucks right outside baggage claim.

How's that for a comeback?

Beyond the Usual

Another one to most definitely avoid is Times Square on New Year's Eve. Or even the Halloween Day parade in the village. (Because it's televised, do the smart thing, will ya? Avoid the high school crowds and watch it at home instead.) Get my point? On New Year's Eve most New Yorkers are either out of town or have house parties as little dinner soirees (and by that I mean takeout Chinese food with cheap wine). The same mindset goes to the Fourth of July, except we're either out of town or have little parties on someone's marvy roof deck.

> **Note:** *How's this for irony? Once you're a New Yawker, you'll tend to avoid things you perhaps previously dreamed about, like checking out the Macy's Thanksgiving Day Parade. Newsflash for ya: Forget the parade; you'll be drenched with tourists, it could perhaps rain or be cold, and there are better views on television. The true magic lies in the blowing up of the floats on Thanksgiving Eve, anyway. Three simple words to remember: Upper. West. Side.*

You'll slowly start peeling back New York City like an onion, a multifaceted onion that will sometimes move you to tears with its majesty. *(So not kidding.)* And truth be told, a lot of the magic is free, free, free! Why not go to Grand Central Station in the middle of rush hour and marvel at the giant American flag and tons and tons of commuters who all seem to be running in zigzag formations? Or how about going to the rooftop deck of the Metropolitan Museum of Art during the summer on Friday nights right after you've enjoyed some of the classical music, a la violins? Rooftop decks are extremely popular in Manhattan during the summer months. Who wouldn't want to be outside in a social setting dancing against the skyline?

Even an expensive cocktail at 230 Fifth (literally, the address is 230 Fifth Avenue) will be worth the bird's-eye view of its next-door neighbor, the Empire State Building. Let's not forget strolling through Bergdorf's on Fifth Avenue just for kicks. Or getting lost among the cobblestone streets in the West Village before sitting down for a bite to eat in Pastis, one of the places that's great to see and be seen.

Marvel in Its Majesty

As for other gems? My absolute fave is the National Arts Club in Gramercy. Sure, you need to be a member or know someone who is a member in order to enter. But that, my friend, adds to its charm and allure. The interior is stunning—ranging from the immense paintings to antiquated books—as is its illustrious history. University Clubs are always magical, too. Whether it's the Harvard Club, the Yale Club, the Williams Club, or the Princeton Club, among others, chances are if you mix and mingle with a variety of folks, eventually you'll get invited to an event at one of these establishments, like a cocktail party or interesting lecture. Do not pass it up! It's oh-so chic in an old-school, academic kind of way.

Another cerebral experience is checking out the grandiose main branch of the New York Public Library on Fifth Avenue and 41st. Yep, the one with two lions, Patience and Fortitude, out front (yes, their names actually date back to the Great Depression; and secondly, it's such a photo op!). The inside halls beckon you like a beaux arts museum and you can even bring your laptop and update your resume (or pretend to update it and update your Facebook status instead, hehe) in one of the majestic rooms. Fancy that!

Expect the Unexpected

Of course, there are the unexpected serendipitous moments that require you to simply pause and nod in disbelief as you punctuate it with a huge smile, "Only in New York!" Like even tonight before I finished up this chapter, there was a bride and groom in a pedi-cab downtown on Irving Place (the bicycle-like cabs that fit only two people, whereby the driver is literally cycling around town). I'm not just saying it was a little moment like, "Oh how cute, check out the bride and groom on their special day." Rather, the newlyweds were followed by the wedding party, wedding guests, and a 10-piece brass band—all on foot! Stopped traffic, they did, as everyone dining at the nearby Pete's Tavern took a moment to applaud the spectacle and marching band's tunes.

You'll shake your head in disbelief when you see a psychotic man uttering things to himself, running at 10 p.m. along Broadway wearing nothing but a woman's black leotard. (So true! Would I even dare to make this stuff up?) Or how about the uneasy feeling you'll get when something scary happens like seeing a highly inebriated man on the subway tracks (note I didn't say *platform;* I said *tracks*) on West 4th? Luckily, more than one citizen informed the subway attendant. I think they stopped the trains and got the man off the track—at least I would hope they did. I didn't stay to see the outcome. But alas, I digress.

Net net: As soon as you step outside your apartment, anything can happen; and rest assured, it will. If you need just one more example, last year the Pope was in town. Yes, the one and only Pope. I went for a walk with a friend and happened to be walking on a street that was closed off. Wouldn't ya know it? I had my camera and poof! A few moments later the NYPD drove by with a few cars and then yes, a car drove by with the Pope nestled inside as a passenger. I'm convinced that magical moments like this happen only in New York!

You'll need to be alert at all times. But take the good with the bad, the glorious to the gross to the OMG, for real? Gawd, I love New Yawk.

Lovin' Your New Metropolis

Each neighborhood in Manhattan is so distinctly different from the next that oftentimes it appears to be a lot of charming little villages connected to make up the big picture of the island. Ahhhhh. While it's important to enjoy everything New York City has to offer in terms of the sights and such, it's just as important to get immersed as a local. As you're touring NYC like a visitor, it's time to get down to business like you mean it. Like you live here. Like you own it. Technically, you do!

When TV anchor and author Tamsen Fadal relocated to NYC from Philly, she got in touch with the locals. Having already moved around the country a lot, she knew the best way to get settled into her new life was to connect with the community. "Instead of going to the Statue of Liberty and Empire State Building, I joined the local gym." Anytime she saw something she had a remote interest in, she got out of her apartment and went. People dine here all the time by themselves and go to the theater all alone, so if you're hung up on relying on someone, get over it.

She says, "If you're moving to New York, you have to be a little daring and a little bold when you get out there." Of course, moving to

Manhattan can be scary and lonely at first, and it can indeed be hard. It doesn't have to be. Tamsen recommends letting friends and family members know where you're going to be—now it's easier than ever, given all the social networking that's going on online. Moving to Manhattan, anyone there? "You have to be open to new experiences and meeting new people," she said.

Of course as you can probably guess, there are pockets of Manhattan you'll simply have to discover on your own. That is part of the joy of living here and the pain of never truly getting to discover it all! This is where you will indeed enter time into the equation. Remember during your job search when we threw the clock out of the window and left it up to the universe to decide your career fate? When it comes to discovering Manhattan, you'll have to make it a priority in terms of time or it'll just slip away from you.

Who knows, after living here a few years you may get transferred out of town with your job, or you may have countless business trips that leave you New York–less for quite a while. Or you may go back to grad school in another state. Whatever the scenario, although Manhattan will be here forever, perhaps you won't be (perish the thought!). This is why it's important to make a list of every cool place you want to check out within the first 12 months of your arrival. I know, I know, I totally broke that rule with my four years to check out Ellis Island, but apparently life is what happens when you're busy making other plans (or so said John Lennon).

You'll need to smell the roses in a big way; and in due time, you'll become in-the-know all on your own. Whether you have brunch at Pete's Tavern on Irving Place, grab a burger and yummy frozen custard at the Shake Shack in Madison Square Park, or meet up with your roommate at the local Crumbs cupcakery for an after-work treat, it's all fabulous, darling. Simply fabulous.

Note: *Pete's Tavern is the city's longest continuously operating bar and restaurant. It opened in 1864, and not even Prohibition forced it to close down! It was disguised as a flower shop during that time. (Neat, eh?)*

Reason #899,999 why I love this town: Where else but New York City would a hamburger stand

+ Have its own Web site?

+ Have a webcam onsite so you can see how long the lines are?

The Shake Shack, that's who.

Cupcakes 101

Manhattan is known for its hot dog street vendors, hot pretzels, countless ethnic restaurants, and one more must-have calorie-infested delicacy: cupcakes! The biggest trend is here to stay; they're everywhere, ranging from high-end swanky parties right down to preschoolers' playdates. Here are the top three, according to moi:

+ **Buttercup Bake Shop:** Nestled in Midtown West and the Upper West Side, this cupcakery was founded by the original owner of Magnolia. And don't be fooled: Their cupcakes aren't the only to-die-for things on the menu.

+ **Crumbs Bake Shop:** My personal fave, this bake shop originally opened its doors in '03 in the UWS and hasn't looked back since. They now ship to practically all parts of the country and have popped up in countless neighborhoods in Gotham—and now the Hamptons and the 'burbs, too! (My fave is the cappuccino cupcake with its supersized frosting. And the funny thing is, I don't even like coffee!)

+ **Magnolia:** Made famous from a scene in *Sex and the City,* this West Village old-time bakery is quite the confectioner's experience! It's all in their icing. Come to mama, sweet sugar! They now have locations in Midtown West and the Upper West Side. And thank goodness for that; the WV location officially feels like a tourist spot, bouncer and all.

Reason #900,000: You gotta love bakeries that stay open past midnight! Late-night munchies gotcha down? Go to Magnolia in the village!

Culture Shock!

Here's yet another lesson in tough love coming straight at ya, sassy girl. This goes back to the Introduction, when we first met and I asked you if you truly had New York in you. And assuming you do (because why else would you keep on reading?), you gotta adjust to the grid or get out. The concrete jungle. The idea of feeling trapped.

Since you won't have a car, nor will you drive one for months and months, you'll soon realize how cumbersome it would be to have one. It's a huge financial burden, it's not necessary, and hey, who wants to move a car every other day when alternate-side street parking is in effect? You'll deal with walking long city blocks in the frigid temps or winter or handle the guy with pickle breath standing way too close to you on the subway knowing that having a car here is simply not an option.

During the sweltering summer months you'll arrive at your office drenched in sweat because those subway platforms might as well be 110 degrees. Oh yeah, as if you needed a reminder, everything is expensive, including the city and state taxes. It's not cheap, so you might as well live like a rock star, yes?

In chapter 11 you'll meet Aaron, a super-savvy 20-something mover and shaker. He says if you're going to fail in New York City, you'll get the signals pretty fast. And girl, is he right. "This is the place to be at the top of your game!" You have to put yourself out there, surround yourself with confident people. So, if you're flailing about at work, your clients, your boss, your co-workers, somebody will let you know. If your social skills need to be brushed up, you'll most definitely get the hint. "The only people in NYC should be the ones who love it. It's not personal, it's all business."

This is what I love about New Yorkers: We're to the point. Direct, no beating around the bush. We're also not mean-spirited or rude, contrary to the stereotype. I know I'm biased but come on, now! There are tons of kind people here; you just need to be open to realizing they do exist. Awww, group hug.

That's a Wrap

As you embrace your new home by seeing the sights of the city and getting a feel for it, guess what happens next? You'll continue exploring and will feel more accustomed to its vibe, its sights (dare I even say, its smells?). After checking out museums and having more than your share of cupcakes, you'll slowly become in the know. That's right, you will become an expert at appreciating New York City and all its splendors, not to mention exploring new nooks and crannies. Consider this your rookie year as you're on your way to an MVP status.

As all rookies experience inevitable ups and downs during their "freshman" year, just remember that you will, too. If you find out that you're faltering, reach out to your inner circle. Be open to constructive criticism and heed their advice. Dealing with the move is one thing, as we talked about in chapter 9. Moving onward and upward is certainly another!

Hey, we're New Yorkers: We don't apologize; we simply do not care what you think about us. If you want to develop your own self-induced inferiority complex, go right ahead. We simply don't care. By this point we're already moving forward with our next yummy lunch/dinner/cocktails plans.

Celeb Sightings

Like, OMG! Yes, you, too, will have your share of celebrity sightings in the city that never sleeps. My first one was spotting Woody Allen just walking on the sidewalk. And a week later I saw pop singer JoJo headed into Dylan's Candy Bar right near Bloomie's. I always cringe when people say to expect the unexpected; but in this case, they're so right. You'll never know when you'll walk past random stars on the street or see them exiting a hotel or perhaps on the treadmill next to you. As for the best places to easily spot a celeb without too much effort? Try the Waverly Inn in the West Village, Pastis (also in the Village), and the Rose Bar in the Gramercy Park Hotel.

Takeout: Resources to Go

Books

Newcomer's Handbook for Moving to and Living in New York City (Stewart Lee Allen)

Not for Tourists: New York City (Jane Pirone)

Shecky's Dirt Cheap NYC (Jean Tang)

Web Sites

Big Onion Walking Tours: www.bigonion.com

Buttercup Bake Shop: www.buttercupbakeshop.com

Crumbs Bake Shop: www.crumbs.com

Ellis Island: www.ellisisland.org/genealogy/ellis_island_visiting.asp

Grand Central Terminal: www.grandcentralterminal.com

Magnolia Bakery: www.magnoliabakery.com

Lincoln Center: www.lincolncenter.org

New York Public Library: www.nypl.org

Theatre Development Fund (Broadway Tickets): www.tkts.com

CHAPTER 11

GET A SIZZLIN' SOCIAL LIFE

I t's truly phenomenal that you've made it this far on the journey, and so pause and pat yourself on the back! Okay, now you've nailed the job, landed the apartment, dealt with rough patches, and learned to truly navigate the ins and outs of New York City. Therefore, it's inevitable you will want to meet new friends! The next step in living off the vibe of New York is to become social and take a huge, juicy bite out of the Big Apple.

The good news: There are countless ways to meet a ton of cool people in Gotham. The bad news? It could literally be overwhelming, girl! Lucky you; I'm here to help you.

Getting Started Making New Friends

First things first: Let's go with the most obvious. If you've already landed a job or if you're still crashing on your cousin's couch, work it. Invite yourself to tag along with the initial social connections you have already made. Don't feel shy about it! You can even say something like, "Do you mind if I tag along? That party sounds like it will be a lot of fun!"

Be sure to make use of your good ol' reliable networks as you're in the process of establishing the foundation for your new one. When you start laying the foundation brick by brick, you'll slowly start to naturally make friends and it won't seem so daunting or on your to-do list in big letters like, "Make Friends." Okay, I know you're not that dorky, but once you start working you'll notice that friendships will automatically start to emerge.

How Chummy Should You Be with Co-workers?

Leah Beirne in Brooklyn made solid friends through an old job. Although she no longer works in her old job, Leah makes it a priority to keep in touch with her old work pals. This alum of New York University worked in ad sales at the magazine *Time Out New York Kids*. Well, she and her co-workers spent most of their time planning which tony events they could try and go to for free, as well as planning lunches! Leah notes that in the end they all loved each other. "We saw each other through countless breakups, deaths, illnesses, hung-over days, etc."

Although she no longer sees her work buddies every single day, they are still some of her closest friends, having bonded over various things like playing with bouncy balls all over the office when a company sent about 100 promotional bouncy balls to their office digs. "We took to bouncing them all over the office. It's a lofted office and we were on the top level, so if they bounded out of control they would end up in production or photo. We called it Urban Bouncy."

This begs the question: Where should you draw the line with co-workers? Should you become friends to the point where you share intimate details of your life or keep the line firmly intact? The best rule of thumb is to become friendly but not too close. Friendships often blossom after co-workers no longer work together; after all, this is New York. There could be cattiness and cutthroat behavior in particular depending on the job. It wouldn't be uncommon, let's say, if you were in ad sales like Leah and other people tried to take your accounts as their own. "You just had to be tough and say, 'THIS IS MINE,'" notes Leah. "No one else is looking out for your commission but you."

Scavenger Hunts in the City

Friendships may emerge as a result of team-building exercises in the form of boat cruise outings, dinners, and yes, even scavenger hunts! Yes, that type of scavenger hunt. You know the drill; you recall it all too well. Sure, in your sorority perhaps you had to borrow a composite photo from a nearby fraternity house. But in the big baddie Big Apple, anything goes.

The purpose of a recent scavenger hunt within a publishing company was to build camaraderie among sales execs. In Manhattan there are a plethora of serious options like dinner, a show, or a boat cruise around the island (or all of the above). As for this team, they had two hours to accomplish as many things on the list as they could. Whether it was taking a picture of someone in a Red Sox (banish the thought!), Yankees (hooray!), and Mets (be that as it may) cap or taking a pic of the grandiose clock in Grand Central Station, it was all in good Gotham fun. Another task was sitting in chairs in the pedestrian mall in Times Square. As for another? Taking a pic with the doorman at the Empire State Building. And yet another, some co-workers served ice cream in the Mr. Softie truck out and about the city. Bonus points were given if you and your team drove a pedestrian cab down Fifth Avenue.

So, my point (and I do have a few): Work-related things, even meetings, don't have to be B to the ORING in all caps. Infuse them with a little fun, why don't ya?! Imagine this: Your co-workers may actually be cool, and as years go by you'll be guaranteed to be invited to some of their weddings and vice versa. And secondly, New York City is at your fingertips. Aside from having monster skyline views in a kickin' board room, there are tons of perks to working in a city like Manhattan. The scavenger hunt and the overall creativity involved with it is merely one of them.

Keep Some Things to Yourself

In addition to cutthroat aspects on the job, it's in your best interest to keep personal things personal. The last thing you want is office gossip circulating about your weekend escapades. While you certainly see your work family more than your roommate and other friends you don't work with, the line must be drawn again when it comes to Facebook.

You know where I'm going with this, don'tcha? Leah learned from her Stern School friends back in '05 to literally un-tag possibly damaging photos of herself since employers were starting to look at them. "At the time most of our drinking photos were tagged when we were not of age, so we were very concerned." Plus, do you really want all your co-workers knowing your personal biz'ness? Knowing where you'll be after work if you RSVP to certain events? This is where privacy settings come into play. While you will certainly see a few friendships at work flourish and have the opportunity to meet cool people, you should also always have your guard up. Instead of being paranoid, just be smart about it. If you wouldn't want your photo, status update, or anything from FB printed on the cover of the *New York Times,* simply delete it.

Marshan Purnell, Former Retail Goddess and Travel Addict

When Marshan originally moved to New York City from Florida, the aspiring CPA played the Buffy card. That's right: She forged alumnae connections with her sorority! "Joining my online sorority chapter helped in meeting good, quality friends here in the city, which is hard to do." She says, "At the end of the day you want to know there are people nearby that care about you and are there to listen or celebrate your big news. So thank goodness for Delta Zeta or I would have missed out on meeting some great people in the city."

This is why networking is your friend. You can never have too many friends or make too many connections. Marshan also joined a women's networking group called the Step Up Women's Network and made friends through it. "That has been great for networking. I never leave an event without getting at least one woman's business card and then I send my resume within 24 hours."

The Snowball Effect

Anything goes! In a city that never sleeps with countless ways to meet people from all walks of life, you never know what your friendships will bring. When Andrew Der, a director of marketing, moved to the city, he hung out with friends who had already been living here. "The more I went out, the more I met people." Plus, he volunteered in the marketing department of a local magazine, so that helped him meet new people. Get this: One of the first few people he met and became friends with after moving to Gotham was a guy from the Village People! (Yes, as in those Village People: "It's fun to stay at the Y-M-C-A...")

"I think one of my favorite things about New York City is the accessibility and variety of people you meet. One of the first few people I met and became friends with when I moved here was the original cowboy from the Village People, Randy Jones." As for the back story? Andrew met Randy at a party. He recalls it was probably through volunteering at *Next Magazine*.

Among other notable friendships, Andrew became really good friends with the person who was the inspiration for Madonna's *Vogue* video. Andrew was at a bar and he noticed his friend was talking to Willi Ninja. Assuming they were friends, he went up to Willi and introduced himself. They became good friends after that; but unfortunately, Willi passed away in September 2006. Andrew explains, "Through Willi I met a bunch of random people I never would have met, like Jay Alexander and Nole Marin from *America's Next Top Model* and Benny Ninja and Patricia Field. It's amazing how so many groups of people are interconnected."

Net net: In NYC you'll get to meet people who live fascinating lives and have experienced so much. It's a great learning experience, really. There's always someone doing something amazing and awe inspiring. It makes you want to step up your game, yes?

That's the key to thriving in NYC: You need to be open to new friendships since you never know who you'll meet. You wouldn't have had the burning desire to move to Gotham if you didn't want a snazzy little life to make everyone back at home jealous, now would ya? You signed up for the gig, and stellar people will come into your life if you let 'em. I can honestly say that I've met a songwriter for a popular J. Lo song, tons of celebs (due to interviewing them for my work), the woman who wrote the *Cheetah Girls* books, funky DJs, and so on. Everyone has a story, whether it's hanging out with a former New York Yankees ballplayer at Rare (a fantastic restaurant) in Murray Hill or like mine when Martha Stewart was behind me checking in at a fashion show. Since check-in was alphabetical by last name, it was a no-brainer she was there. And no, I did not let her cut in line.

> **Note:** *When you're out and about in the social swirl, managing your schedule without overdoing it may be a challenge since you'll be meeting tons of people and they can quickly take up valuable real estate on your calendar. Through the process of elimination and simply showing up to events and get-togethers, you'll be able to realize who falls into the acquaintance category and who doesn't.*

Another way to make friends is to buy them. (Kidding, of course!) But you really do need to get out of your apartment and put effort into it. If you pursue activities you enjoy doing, chances are you'll also meet others in the process. Unlike in the 'burbs, you won't be surrounded by teenyboppers or thirtysomethings with 2.2 kids, the minivan, and the white picket fence. Rather, you can easily find people with similar interests and rock them out. It's quite empowering, too, when you hear other people's stories.

"Be Nice to Everyone"

Meet Aaron Hager, who works at a fragrance company. The savvy social guy lived off credit cards for the first two months he moved to Manhattan. After initially moving into the Chelsea Hotel, he knew that in the worst-case scenario if things didn't work out, he could have always moved back home. "Would you rather be $10,000 in debt or miserable and not see any future? I'd rather be in debt. New York has so much to offer if you're willing to accept it."

With an attitude like, "If you feel like you're going to do well, you'll do well," he certainly has. "Be nice to people. How you treat them is how you'll be treated back," he says. Social skills will serve you well, even if it's waiting in line outside the Waverly Inn to get in or trying to get into the uberphenomenal Rose Bar at the Gramercy Park Hotel. "Go anywhere successful people hang out and strike up a conversation.

It's all about being in the moment. You have to be confident to get in. It's a great equalizer: You can't get in; neither will they." For instance, when you're waiting outside the venue with velvet ropes, why not strike up a positive conversation with other people around you? Seize the moment and have fun with it. Rather than bemoan the fact that you're still outside, why not talk about how you're looking forward to getting in or make a joke about how funny it is to have tons of bars and clubs in the city without a queue and yet be waiting outside for this sizzlin' one in particular? Be confident that you belong there and have faith that you will get in eventually. (The worst-case scenario if you don't get in? You made a new friend waiting on line.) As you're surrounded by other people who are getting their social game on, regardless of whether they're a CEO or administrative assistant, playing the waiting game to get in means you're all on the same wavelength, at least at that moment in time.

In the end, your success, happiness, and not to mention social life, is all about building relationships. "The outcome of meeting someone at the top is going to be so much better than meeting someone at the bottom." Go where successful people hang out and learn from them. Aaron's story in a nutshell is quite invigorating as work and social lives intertwine.

The alum of Bowling Green University studied apparel merchandising and product development and also transferred to FIT in NYC during his stint at Bowling Green. While at FIT he focused on advertising and marketing/communication. Well, in a New York minute he met Betsey Johnson and was offered an internship that very same night! "I took it all in when I went to school. That's when I fell in love with NYC."

At the end of the first semester he landed another internship. Instead of filing or getting someone lunch, he learned hands-on sales skills from Janine Weil. "She taught me the ins and outs of showroom sales." Instead of being comfortable with the big-name internship, he wanted to work harder, and work he did! "With the effort you put into NYC you'll see your progress quickly. What you put into it is what you get out of it."

Fast forward: Aaron temped a lot and did a lot of different jobs while working as the concierge at a hotel, making a ton of connections. As for his current job for NEST fragrances in the home fragrance industry, Aaron found it through craigslist. His parting words? "Be nice to everyone." You said it, brotha!

Fleeting Friends

Whether you're connecting with new peeps via organizations or even waiting on line behind the barricaded red-carpet ropes, keep in mind that friendships will stray. This is why it's super important that your ability to easily meet new people remain sharp, intact, and always in practice. As fun as it is getting to know new people and gallivanting to their birthday parties, brunches, and cupcake dates, don't get too comfy. Although people may be open to having you join their circles (chances are, they were in your shoes a few years ago, too), the landscape will change. *All. The. Time.*

Just when you think you've met some super-fly quality people with similar goals and viewpoints, the rug will be pulled out from under you. Someone you thought was fantastic may end up turning into a total beeotch; others will get engaged, while others move away (perish the thought). As for the good news? New people are constantly moving to the metropolis as well. This is the physical movement as it relates to friends, but there's always the spiritual element, too. You'll likely evolve as will they. Friendships drift apart while others get stronger. This is a given.

Valentina Afanasii reminds you to have the expectation that you'll need to continuously put effort into your friendships. "If you establish a group of friends or a network at some point, you can't rely that it will stay like that forever," she says. Yes, this means people will come in and out. Just consider it a revolving door at Bloomindale's on Lex (as in Lexington Avenue). Sometimes it'll move fast, and other times pretty slow. Just be sure to realize that movement is inevitable.

"You need to renew that circle and keep using it over and over in terms of meeting new people and making new friends," she adds. And what's a better place to do that than in New York City? As you become more grounded in who you are in Manhattan and when identifying new friends, the landscape of your friendships at home or with college buddies may change, too. Do not be dismayed, my friend. This is normal and is part of the maturing process.

Fun Groups

By now I've covered the basics of friends, so I'll simply dive into a variety of ways to expand your social circle. Here's a newsflash and not-so-subtle reminder: In Gotham you gotta leave your apartment if you want to create a life. I know, I know, it sounds a bit basic, yet it can be overwhelming. There is so much going on so you'll end up with too many options. And hey, with perhaps Netflix at your fingertips and takeout Chinese food, sometimes a night in could be very tempting. (Actually, this is perfectly acceptable on a Saturday night so as to avoid the B&T crowd; but on weeknights, diva, the city is your oyster! Go and grab it!)

The Lunch Club

Anyway, in Manhattan it's normal that if you want to try a restaurant and have no one to dine with, you go alone. You know what? You become pretty darn self-sufficient. You'll go by yourself with a book or newspaper to keep you company. You'll learn to appreciate a lot about a restaurant this way. Anyway, Jared Nissim founded an organization based on just that: Eating alone, but together.

Jared worked as a full-time freelance writer from home way back in 2001. After experiencing the oddities of having complete freedom yet feeling isolated, he wanted to increase his daytime interaction with New Yorkers. The result? He created a community, The Lunch Club (www. TheLunchClub.com), with all sorts of events ranging from speed friending (think speed dating but insert potential friends instead of prospective dates) to bartending classes to scavenger hunts in Grand Central Station! It all began when he placed an ad on craigslist to see if other freelancers in the East Village wanted to meet up. And voilà! The very first Lunch Club event took place at Café Mogador on St. Marks between 1st and Avenue A. His Web site has become a mecca of social activity in terms of upcoming events in Manhattan and the nearby boroughs. You don't have to go to every single event, silly. Just log on and see what suits your fancy among the affordably priced outings and you're guaranteed to meet some new peeps!

Meetups and Tweetups

This brings up another point: Meetups! They're all over the city. Looking for some entrepreneurial pursuits? Find other entrepreneurs via Meetups. Dying to find some Cleveland Indians fans in the Big Apple? Meet up. I could go on and on, but let it suffice to say that there are gatherings in a plethora of categories. Meetups are yet another way to get out there.

If you're into social networking, Tweetups may be up your alley as well. The beauty of Twitter-inspired parties is there's almost always a nametag. Not only are nametags a terrific way to break the ice; in Twitterville, instead of writing your real name, you'll write your Twitter "handle." Perhaps your real name is Melissa but your Twitter alias is @NewCityGal. Nevertheless, you can find out about these events (usually held in a bar in the form of a happy hour) via Twitter, in particular the 12for12K challenge, which aims to have charitable events every month in a different city. Check out www.12for12k.org for more information.

ZogSports

If athletic co-ed events are more up your alley, you may want to check out ZogSports (www.zogsports.org), a charity-focused coed social sports club among young professionals in Manhattan, Brooklyn, Queens, and apparently now in Hoboken, too. The intramural league was created after 9/11 when its founder, Robert Herzog, had a close call. He was running late for work and tardiness saved his life. His office was located on the 96th floor of World Trade I; and sadly, none of Robert's co-workers got out of the building alive that horrific morning. The grave situation gave him impetus to take stock of his life. As such, he decided to build upon human charity he witnessed post-9/11 and foster community in New York. ZogSports is merely one sports league example. The key is finding things you enjoy doing and seeking ways to do them with others. It's quite simple, yes? For instance, there are a bunch of running clubs in Manhattan.

> **Note:** *Oh yeah, the marathon in November is a huge event. HUGE in all caps huge. If you have no intentions to ever run unless perhaps you're trying to chase a bus you just missed, never fear. Marathon Sunday is a very big social event! Whether you get invited to a friend's apartment for morning cocktails or go with a bunch of people to carry signs and cheer on the runners, it's all good.*

Non-athletic groups are everywhere, too! See, you just need to start searching and all of a sudden it will be like the time you went to the activity fair in college and signed up for everything: too many activities, too little time.

Women's Groups

There's the Step Up Women's Network (www.suwn.org), which I totally recommend! Step Up is a national nonprofit membership organization that strengthens community resources for women and girls. Through teen empowerment programs for underserved girls, women's health education and advocacy, professional mentorship, and social networking opportunities, there are tons of events that may interest you. Membership fees are affordable and there's typically an open-house event every November, but you don't have to wait 'til that event to enroll as a member.

You may also want to check out The Women's Mosaic (www.thewomensmosaic.org), a cool organization dedicated to uniting and empowering women through programs that promote intercultural understanding and personal growth.

Alumni Groups

Another way to spice up your social life is to get back to your roots. Let's not forget about alumni events! What better way to connect on common ground than to meet fellow alums? You'll have that bond as an instant conversation starter, even if you didn't know them on campus.

Now, let's think outside the box, diva! You can always go to alumni events where you did not—I repeat, did *not*—go to school. Duke

University's alumni "hoop watches" are pretty big here in Gotham, as are certain telecasts of big football games for Michigan. Feel free to crash them! Hey, if you want to get your party and work-the-room game face on, you gotta think outside your social comfort zone.

Divas Who Dine

If alumni lectures or basketball game happy hours aren't your cup of green tea, let's go back to the glam! I'm a big fan of Divas Who Dine (www.divaswhodine.com). Dedicated to helping fashionable, fabulous women who work in media, fashion, hospitality, and related fields "make it happen," the organization provides a super-fab way to network. You can literally bring a stack of business cards and expect to get a stack in return. I've never left an event without having had really good conversations and later seeing friendships emerge.

Community Service

Tired of this long list? Don't you worry, it keeps growing. Cultural events are also another option, as is one huge one: community service! As you volunteer you'll feel good giving back to the community. Whether it's Habitat for Humanity, the Red Cross, Big Brothers/Big Sisters, or New York Cares (www.nycares.org/volunteer, an organization mobilizing New Yorkers), there are countless ways to volunteer in the big city.

Make the Effort and Get Involved

A key to the whole let's get a life in New York concept is this: You gotta put in effort and you gotta follow up. Face time is crucial and so is being focused. If you run all over the place to random wine tastings or an alumni event here or a sporting event there, sure you may have fun. But guaranteed you'll be exhausted, and you won't make true, solid, consistent connections. I've found the best way to feel like a big fish in a small pond (trust me, sistah, it can and will be done in due time) is to join organizations, get involved on specific committees, and show up.

Remember when you became an officer in your sorority, became a campus tour guide, or worked on the school newspaper? You probably attended meetings, felt more involved, got back what you gave, and felt like a face as you walked across campus and occasionally bumped into people from said organizations. You can get that same warm 'n' fuzzy feeling as you get connected and plugged into Gotham.

Mix It Up

Another strategy to get out there and make connections while having fun is to mix it up. If your New York personality is pretty literary, why not go to The Cutting Room, a lounge and music club in the Flatiron District, to hear a new eclectic rock band one night? If you're into sports, why not go to Chelsea Piers, a sports and entertainment complex on the west side between 17th and 23rd, to see if you can join an adult ice hockey league?

Braniac, as much as your interests could be one way today, tomorrow they could be totally different; and actually, they should be. By diversifying your endeavors, you'll totally meet a new crew of people. Feel free to punk it up or professional it down when the occasion arises. If you're attending a fantastic lecture to hear Mario Batali speak at the 92nd Street Y, why not sign up for cooking classes downtown? Or why not put on your best Martin Scorsese and enroll in a film production class at The New School?

While we're free-associating, there's always the Learning Annex (www.learningannex.com). Yeah, they have classes available online, but since the goal is getting out there and meeting people, whether it's a class on real estate or quirky topics like how to make money doing voiceovers, you'll want to actually attend their classes in person. While their classes are typically one-offs (as in one night for a few hours and you're done), your chances of meeting people will likely increase if the class meets multiple times, such as foreign-language classes at the 92nd Street Y.

As you gallivant to and from various classes and events, there's also Shecky's Girls Night Out. For a cover charge, you can go to this evening event held a few times each year full of shopping, cocktails, beer and food pairings, beauty treatments, and goody bags.

Go Glam: Get Your Party On

As far as partying it up goes, can I get a whoop whoop? Manhattan has tons of bars to suit every need (swanky like Cipriani's to sweaty frat boy a la Brother Jimmy's and back again!), lounges, dance clubs, and music venues. The social scene is not lacking, as you can imagine, so in order to not burn yourself out (and by that I mean your wallet), examine your budget and frequently check in with your energy level so that you don't over-schedule. If the Met has an amazing exhibit you plan on checking out with a new friend during a Sunday morning along with brunch, you will not want to party it up at Nikki Beach in Midtown 'til 3 a.m. the evening before. Just sayin'.

Keep in mind that the social life applies to weeknights only. If you've been paying attention, and I sincerely hope you have, you've learned by now that the weekends are reserved for tourists and the B&T crowd. Yes, that means you'll hang out with friends for Monday Night Football or you'll go to happy hours on Thursdays; but when Saturday night rolls around, you'll be nestled in a small birthday party gathering or Netflix fiesta.

Add all of the above to special events that occur in the city and they can be amazing, scintillating, and downright draining! Invites tend to get more invites, that's for sure. Case in point: Perhaps your friend in advertising is sponsoring an after party during Fashion Week. Well, you can guess what happens next: You're chatting it up with an adorable intern from an up-and-coming fashion house—and lo and behold, you get invited to their fashion show for the spring line. While you're there, you are friendly yet again and talk to a publicist repping a new band that is being played by the fashion show's DJ. Lo and behold, a listening party is in your future! Isn't this fun? I heart Manhattan. Ahhhhh.

Note: *If you're thinking you need to hire a personal assistant to keep up with your happenin' social calendar, hooray! You are well on your way to a super-fly social life. Hey, if I wasn't already livin' the dream, I'd be jealous of you.*

Special Events

As if all of this isn't enough, there are special events occurring through-out the year, too. The Jacob Javits Center often holds events that are open to the public throughout the year and are free, free, free! For instance, their camera show in October is free to the public since exhib-itors are the ones paying megabucks to attend. They have photo classes (you may have to pay for specific ones, so don't quote me on that). But the point is, depending on the event, you can check out Javits. The Chocolate Show occurs in November and the Westminster Kennel Club Dog Show happens in February. (Totally random that they're in the same sentence, but whatever; you get the idea.)

Sports

Let's not forget about sports! There are the Yankees and Mets, Knicks, Nets, Lady Liberty, Rangers, Devils, and Islanders. There are sporting events throughout the year like the U.S. Open Tennis tournament every summer in Queens. If bowling is your schnizzle, there's always Bowlmor Lanes. Since sporting events with friends may be a blast, it's highly unlikely you'll specifically make new friends there. But alas, if you're looking to go bowling or tap into a league, glow-in-the-dark bowling with big-screen video walls and a thumping sound system give you a reason to yell, "Strike!" (Okay, please don't tell me you'll actu-ally be one of those people to say it aloud; but suffice it to say you'll get to wear funky-smelling bowling shoes for the evening and enjoy a full service restaurant serving lane-side.)

How to Work the Room in Three Simple Steps

1. Show up. Duh, diva. This one is a Big Apple no-brainer!

2. Bring business cards. Plenty of them. My recommendation? Create your own personal business cards online (www. printsmadeeasy.com) instead of bringing your company card. You can simply have it state your name and e-mail address/phone number. After all, do you really want that new hottie you talked to e-mail you to your work e-mail address? It's particularly helpful if you're making new business connections so they associate meeting you with your name and face rather than with your company. Hey, nothing is permanent, so why not start establishing your brand and contact information, which will not likely change?

3. Stand at the bar or near the kitchen if food is circulating. You will be guaranteed to meet people. "Mmmm, these crab cakes are delicious, don't you think?" could very well be a convo starter. Sometimes I think we psyche ourselves out when it comes to small talk. Don't even worry if it sounds cheesy; sometimes all you need is an icebreaker like, "You look familiar. This may sound crazy, but did you go to (insert your university's name here)?"

   And if you're attending a lecture, how about this one: "That was an interesting talk! What did you think about it?" Or, how about going with basic ones like the weather, the Yankees, any pending strike (every few months doormen or MTA public transit people or someone is threatening to strike)... you get the idea. As long as you look approachable with a smile on your face and have kept abreast of current events (yes, perusing CNN.com 15 minutes a day totally counts), you should be good to go!

The Love Life

Ah, the dating scene. Love it or hate it, in New York the landscape changes for your career and social life, so why should dating be any different? Just like meeting new friends, you'll find there's an abundance of opportunities to meet people. As for meeting quality people? Therein lies the challenge.

If you've watched one too many *Sex and the City* episodes, you'll think life imitates art imitates life. You know what, you city slicker, you? You're right. Rather than dish the dating dirt (let's face it, this section could become an entire book in itself!), it simply makes sense to point you towards the experts, so you'll want to devour the "Takeout" list at the end of this chapter.

Random Trivia About Our MAN...

...hattan! The name was derived from the word Manna-hata according to a 1609 log book of an officer on Henry Hudson's yacht (yes, as in that Henry Hudson—as in the Hudson River). In fact, the name Manhata was depicted twice on a 1610 map on the west and east sides of the Hudson. The word Manhattan was translated into "island of many hills."

Online Dating

Of course, experts will dish about the whole online dating thing, whether it's www.match.com, www.Jdate.com, www.eHarmony.com, or others. Just like with friendships, in New York you never know who's open to adding people to their world, so word of caution: This city moves pretty fast.

As for Vic's tips, be sure you approach anything—dating, friendships, work colleagues, anything that involves people—with an open mind. And remember you never get a second chance to make a first impression. Be relaxed, be yourself, and don't try to say or do something just to fit in if it's not "you." And oh yeah, always avoid the topics of religion, politics, and, in this town, the Boston Red Sox.

Face Time

Want to ditch the online dating thing and be out and about in this town? Meet men in Central Park, sports bars, or Barnes & Noble? Good luck with that (just kidding). New York has countless ways to meet people; but the key, of course, is getting out there. You're not going to meet anyone in your apartment! And if you go to events that you enjoy, like a book talk on a specific subject or a cooking class, chances are you'll meet people.

I've always maintained that if you don't meet a potential love interest at an event, no worries. Someone else you meet at said event could be a connection to your guy. Get my drift? Everyone is a connection, although events like going to a Johnnie Walker event or hearing a lecture at one of the university clubs can be hit-or-miss. You'll never know what the crowd is going to be like in terms of sociability or guy/gal ratio.

Many women in New York rely on online dating, but I won't scare you with the ratio (maybe that's 'cuz it's hard to find the actual stats). You know it, the one where there are how many millions of available, successful, amazing women to the too few eligible bachelors?

The Setup

In addition to the online world as well as various places that interest you (like that cooking class or perhaps a Toastmasters meeting or alumni outing), there's always the setup. Ah yes, the blind date! In this day and age, Google is your friend. As your coworker or friend or cousin or whomever sets you up, I'm telling you the importance of googling, just like you would do your homework before an interview! Will this kill any potential excitement or ability to have the conversation flow organically? Perhaps.

Another key to setups is finding out the relationship of the person you're gonna date to the person who is setting you up. How long have they known each other and what do you they about that person other than that they're single? Sure, you'll want the big-picture deets like their occupation and interests, but how about adjectives like honest, thoughtful, and smart?

I've always maintained that when forming friendships, it does not mean you'll have a ton in common just because you're both single. You can guess where I'm headed with this one: Just because he's a single New Yorker and you're a single New Yorker does not mean you'll immediately hit it off. What shared interests do you have? What commonalities can be an ice breaker? It never hurts to show up for a first date to at least be cordial; but if you have nothing in common except a ZIP code, dating this dude may be a total waste of makeup.

The Meetup

Okay, so let's say you're being set up or you're briefly chatting on match.com (no need to go back and forth a lot by writing a novel about your life. Keep it succinct and set up that date), it's time for the meetup. Hooray! Keep it low-maintenance like a coffee shop or out for drinks and keep it short! No need to have the first date drone on and on, even if you're having a blast. Experts recommend cutting it off after about an hour (two at the max). The basics apply: Let him pursue you; and if he doesn't, his loss. You'll find someone else who will.

And now we must pause for a word or two about safety. As you certainly shouldn't reveal your address (simply saying your 'hood is fine like, "Murray Hill"; no need to say 37th and Lex), and you meet up in a public place, you still need to have your savvy game face on. Should you be yourself? Completely. Be relaxed? Most definitely. Be ignorant? Not likely! I wouldn't expect anything less from you, anyway, but let's face it: This is a huge city with a lot of crazies. Be careful about your words, most definitely the actions, and also the drinks. To avoid having your drink drugged by your date, keep an eye on it at all times. When he says he's going to the bar to get a drink, why not mosey on up to the bar as well to join him? When you need to haul to the ladies room, try to finish your drink ahead of time. Better yet, why drink at all? Seltzer with lime is a perfect combo in terms of keeping your wits about you. Have you ever heard the expression "One drink, two drinks, three drinks...floor"?

In addition when you're one-on-one, you'll also need to avoid getting stalked. This one is tough to tackle. New York is so big; but quite honestly, it could be scary. With the Internet and Google, being anonymous no longer has its privileges. There are a few ways to avoid the stalker scenario, so listen up. First of all, don't reveal too much. When you meet someone, again, there's no need to give your specific address. There's no need to tell them your last name, either. Since stalkers are often lunatics, sometimes it's not necessarily something you could have done differently because they may not handle rejection like a normal person. Net net: Keep your guard up at all times and go with your gut. If you feel like you're being stalked, take precautions, like perhaps removing your entire name from the directory at your walkup building. Of course, having a doorman should add an extra level of security.

> **Note:** *As a footnote to the singlistas of Manhattan, finding decent guys and being super smart about the process, we cannot overlook one tiny little topic that comes up time and time again. Yes, I'm talking about the B&T crowd! Most New Yorkers won't even take the PATH (public transportation from NYC to Hoboken and vice versa) for their annual St. Patty's Day parade in early March, so could you imagine dating a guy that's commutable, too? No dice. Is this narrow-minded? Perhaps. Is this ultimately your decision? You bet, so just heed the following words. When it comes to hanging out with someone super cool that you'd like to get to know better, taking 1½ hours to get there may not be an issue. However, if there's not a lot of chemistry and it feels like a hike to either or both parties (technically, he should be visiting you anyway, yes?), it's time to move on. Some divas simply call it "GU"—Geographically undesirable. NEXT!*

That's a Wrap

Considering the endless social options that are literally yours for the taking, one main point to remember is that getting a life in NYC may feel a lot like college—especially if you didn't have a car on campus, since you certainly won't now. Although there are a variety of similarities (for example, the Great Lawn is your new quad, your tiny studio apartment will feel like a dorm room), the main point is this: Just like in college, you'll have the ability to go out every night of the week if you want. (Assuming, of course that you had a life in college. Ha!)

You can easily enrich your mind and soul (bikram yoga is the new en vogue thing here, too). One of the coolest feelings is being out an about in your own 'hood or another one and bumping into someone you know! Yes, it's a big city, but it doesn't have to feel like one. The more you repeatedly attend events where you feel like you belong, the more you will indeed belong. You, my friend, have the power to make things happen and meet fantastic people in the process.

Takeout: Resources to Go

Web Sites

92nd Street Y: www.92y.org

Citysearch: www.newyork.citysearch.com

Divas Who Dine: www.divaswhodine.com

eHarmony: www.eharmony.com

The Javits Center: www.javitscenter.com

JDate.com: www.jdate.com

The Learning Annex: www.learningannex.com

The Lunch Club: www.thelunchclub.com

Match.com: www.match.com

Meetup.com: www.meetup.com

The New School: www.newschool.edu

Prints Made Easy: www.printsmadeeasy.com

Shecky's: www.sheckys.com

Step Up Women's Network: www.suwn.org

The Women's Mosaic: www.thewomensmosaic.org

ZogSports: www.zogsports.org

(CONTINUED)

(*CONTINUED*)

Books

Why Hasn't He Called? New York's Top Date Doctors Reveal How Guys Really Think and How to Get the Right One Interested (Matt Titus and Tamsen Fadal)

Act Like a Lady, Think Like a Man: What Men Really Think About Love, Relationships, Intimacy, and Commitment (Steve Harvey)

How to Shop for a Husband: A Consumer Guide to Getting a Great Buy on a Guy (Janice Lieberman and Bonnie Teller)

The Man Plan: Drive Men Wild...Not Away (Whitney Casey)

CHAPTER 12

SAVING THE BENJAMINS

O kay, this is the chapter full of tough love. I'm not just sayin' love. I'm sayin' tough loooooooooove. The accent's on the letter "o." As in over-the-top expensive, sister!

Repeat after me: "I will experience sticker shock." Carrie and crew had a whole lot of sex and the city. Well, suffice it to say, you'll have sticker shock in the city. Every. Single. Day. Now, we can always choose to succumb to the ridic housing prices, deli sandwiches that will set you back nine bucks (and that's before adding a can of Diet Pepsi and little bag of Baked Lays), and massive taxi rides exceeding 20 bucks. But you know what? We're not that gal.

We're fighters. We're champions. Insert *Rocky* theme music here! Do you feel the power? I can't hear you...do you feel it? There, that's better. This chapter explores the many ways you can squeeze the most out of your almighty dollar.

Save on Groceries

According to Stacy Francis, CFP, CDFA, and founder of Savvy Ladies, an organization dedicated to providing financial education to women in their quest for financial independence, there are many ways to save small and reap big benefits. She says, "Giving up little things on a daily basis can lead to major savings." For starters, you gotta eat. There are only so many sandwiches and freebie lunches you can score on the employer's dime leftover from meetings with the bigwigs. As such, you'll take a jaunt to Gristedes supermarkets and yes, you'll skip down the narrow aisles at D'Agostino grocery stores. And then you'll realize a box of cereal can set you back as much as six bucks.

Lucky for us, Stacy is one savvy lady. Her advice? Shop at Jacks! Officially known as "Jacks 99 Cent Store," there are a few in the city, my fave being the one at 16 E. 40th, right near the public library. They provide a wide range of items that are sold in bulk and cost only 99 cents. Sometimes they're even less than a buck: If you need a quick fixin' of chocolate for example, you can buy a mini Toblerone for 25 cents—under a dollar, yippee, double exclamation points!!

As for the other stores, yes, Manhattan has more than one Whole Foods. Who can forget snazzy gourmet shops like Zabar's & Co. and Citarella? *You* can, dollar diva! Here's one simple word and don't say I never taught ya anything: Chinatown. "All the fruit is at least half the price than in midtown Manhattan," notes Stacy. "Also, fish and meat are less expensive than anywhere else. Plus, it is fun and a great experience walk around in Chinatown to find great deals." Stacy also says you can get a great deal going wine shopping at Trader Joe's. After all, their lines are long for a reason. "People know they get the best deals there. So waiting is worth it."

Get Your Drink On—Cheaper

My friend, this leads us to the next topic: Imbibing! Want a martini? Um, how about 20 bucks at Nobu. Perhaps a beer at Yankee Stadium? Only if you want to shell out nine bucks. When you want a happening social life, keep in mind two things:

+ First of all, you do not need alcohol to have fun (because let's face it: It's so much more fun being sober watching everyone else get sloppy drunk).

+ Secondly, if you do want an occasional drink, designer cocktails or even draft beers will set you back by mucho greenbacks.

> **Note:** *Meeting up for coffee can add up as well; but lucky for us, there are workarounds.*

Listen up, you still with me? Many happy hours offer free drinks to the tune of buy one, get one free with additional steep discounts. So, if they're offering discounts on American beer, don't try to be all fancy and go imported on us, 'k? Do the smart thing and get whatever's offered on the cheap. Other bars offer free appetizers. And if you're lucky, they'll offer both!

Plus, Stacy mentions you can get cultured as you're getting your happy hour on. "Take in some art and free drinks at the many gallery openings around this city!" In addition, you can always snag an invite to a magazine or product launch party if you work in marketing, advertising, or publishing or know someone who does. Although the parties may get old after a while, in the beginning they're fun and free; and yes, you'll often leave with a goody bag of random promotional items. Win-win all around!

Andrew Der, Director of Marketing, futurethink

When he first moved here, Andrew went out. A lot. "Ironically, the more you go out in New York, the fewer things you have to pay for. I saved money by going to parties with open bars and gift bags. There was usually a magazine throwing a party or product launch event at least once a week. It's also helpful if you work for a company where you get discount products or have friends in similar situations."

New York City isn't only a fantastic city, it's a magnificent place to live when you're young. "And it's a city that, if done properly, only gets better the longer you're here. But you have to really want it and be willing to make some sacrifices, in order to live here—at least at first. But once you're here, it's an amazing city, unlike any other. It's truly the center of the universe."

Sure, Manhattan is all glam and a bag of chips, but according to this marketing exec, you need a high tolerance for things when you live in New York. People will be coughing on you while you ride the subway, you'll most definitely live in tiny quarters, and in a word you'll find filth. "You're still

(CONTINUED)

(CONTINUED)

going to see a rat or roach run past you on the sidewalk at night. I've trained myself to look at the sidewalk when I walk down the street. That's one way to tell if someone lives here or not. When they walk, tourists look up; New Yorkers look down."

Although Andrew looks down to avoid walking into roaches or rats, most of us also look at the ground to avoid walking into garbage bags on the street (when it's garbage night there can be piles and piles of them on the sidewalk). Tourists most definitely gawk at the buildings; we're immune to them and simply don't marvel at them and look down rather than up.

Food, Fabulous Food: Going Out to Eat

So, what would drinks and partying be without food? We dished about grocery shopping, but how about eating out and exploring the countless ethnic restaurants this fantabulous city has to offer? You, too, can dine like a foodie; but you know what? You can easily drop 50 bucks or more on a meal out with friends if you're not careful.

There are a few quick tips for eating on a budget without going hungry in the big city.

+ Select a cool, out-of-the-way restaurant that offers some great deals.

+ Surf online to Citysearch (www.newyork.citysearch.com) or Shecky's (www.sheckys.com) for a nightlife guide based on the neighborhood you're looking for.

+ There are always pretheater deals, too, in the theater district (that is, Times Square and its vicinity).

Stacy advises, "Often you can have a three-course feast of food with a free glass of wine for less than 20 dollars. Be a tourist in your own city and buy the latest *Let's Go* travel guide. Some of my favorite and cheapest meals were finds from that book."

There's also a little secret to dining on the cheap in this city. It's called Restaurant Week. Typically held in June and January, several restaurants throughout Manhattan offer steals and deals. I'm talkin' steaks, sushi, chocolate mousse, and everything yummy in between. For instance, participating restaurants will have a fixed-price menu (ahem, like $20.10 to correspond to the year—cha-ching!).

Snacks on Trucks

Tempting and deeeelicious, that's what they are! If you need a little afternoon break with some co-workers or just a jaunt down the block to get a quick pick-me-up in the form of a typical hot pretzel, you may not be able to say no. They're inexpensive but with a whole lot of carbs. Pretzel stands are everywhere, and every now and then you deserve a cheap caloric treat, yes?

New Yorkers have their favorite street foods, and although hot pretzels rank right up there, Mister Softee cones typically top the list. After all, the brand has been a staple for more than 50 years!

Of course, things you don't see in the movies or on television about Gotham include other delicacy trucks like the Dessert Truck (I hear their brownies are to die for!), the Waffle Truck (with Belgian waffles), and of course, the Mud Truck for coffee.

Get Fit on a Budget

In addition to scouring out cheap eats (believe me, they do exist), there's a reason to be glad that restaurants are typically in the stratosphere of your monthly budget. You know why? Imagine eating out all the time. Your waistline would quickly expand, thereby creating a need for another expanding budget—as in buying bigger clothes—or a gym membership! Many Manhattanites are into jogging, rollerblading, or bicycling in the park. But for the not-so-nice-weather activities, a few gyms are indeed hotspots:

✦ Equinox

✦ New York Sports Clubs

✦ Crunch

Considering that most people spend on average between $50 and almost $200 each month on gym memberships, Stacy recommends cheaper alternatives. "Instead, invest in great workout videos or go running and walking."

For real. You can literally walk up and down and all around this city and not even feel like you're exercising! Running to catch a bus? Exercising. Walking cross-town to a meeting in another office? You guessed it: exercising. Often in Manhattan you're running to or fro, constantly watching your watch, and you forget that an object in motion stays in motion. And what better object to burn calories than YOU?

Public Transportation Is Your Friend

This leads to a tiny little detour better known as not having a car. If you think you're gonna have a car in the big city, think again. Sure, you will feel trapped from time to time (which is why it's key to remember all you need to do is hop on the BoltBus to Boston or D.C. for an inexpensive weekend getaway). Having a car equates to having a headache.

It will cost $400 per month or more to park it in a garage. Guaranteed, your friends back home won't be paying that much in rent, let alone paying it on a place to park a car! There are also crazy rules like alternate-side street parking, yada yada yada. (Truth be told, I don't even know what that means other than it's a royal pain because you'll always need to park and re-park your car.) Plus, in this city you totally do not need wheels. You can hop on a bus or subway or simply hoof it. You'll save cash by not having a car (and hey, I didn't even mention car insurance, gas, or costs associated with maintaining your automobile) and a whole lot of agida.

Now, let's not forget that Manhattan is a big island. A very big island. Huge! The subway can take you anywhere pretty much for $2.25. The best option for using the MetroCard a lot is to buy an unlimited ride pass. In fact, your employer may have transit options that enable you to purchase your MetroCard with pre-tax dollars. Sweet!

You'll believe me when you swipe that card for $2.25 (this is the amount at the time of this printing; rest assured it will rise again in the near future, thereby outdating this precious book!) instead of shelling out big bucks for a lofty taxi ride. By the way, taxis start at $2.50 just for stepping into the cab! That doesn't include the amounts incurred as the meter runs while you sit in traffic, conveniently miss red light after red light, and find your cash dwindling en route to your destination.

Now, there is always a case for taking a taxi. When safety is an issue it's a no-brainer. If you haven't thought about your subway curfew, you might want to contemplate it. What is this curfew, you ask? It's the time at which you cut yourself off from the subway. For me it's 11 p.m. I can bear it up until then, and—knock on wood—I've never specifically felt unsafe prior to that. But honestly, I wouldn't want to risk it and put myself in a precarious situation. Then again, others will say you shouldn't have a subway curfew since you should always feel empowered to leave your house at night. It's a personal choice, but something you may want to ponder.

The Unwritten Rules of the Subway

Anyway, there are unwritten rules of riding the subway. One way is to simply push everyone into the middle of the subway car when it's simply too crowded for your little butt to fit. Kidding! Other people tend to push; your role is to unfortunately get squashed and tactfully resist or push back as necessary. Each woman for herself here!

Note: *Gotta love it when Manhattan men try to be chivalrous and hold the door for you, but as for subway doors? Look out, metro riders! During the heat of rush hour they'll race into a subway car as soon as the doors open regardless of who's in their way. You'll immediately get the text message: It's not always ladies first. Be prepared to hold your ground!*

Not all subway cars are created equal. Some feel wider, and sometimes you'll always snag a seat; other times you won't. It's truly a crap shoot. As for the entertainment? There will almost always be some type of street performer on the platform, so consider it part of your $2.25 admission fee. Ha! On the subway itself there will be homeless people chanting something such as this, "I am homeless, I'm not here to harm you. My husband lost his job, I lost my job and we need money for food. I ask you to open your heart and your wallet…" Blah, blah, blah. This is where people really adhere to the rule of avoiding eye contact. Do some people give spare change? You bet. But, you can imagine that if you opened your wallet every time a homeless person asked for money, you would soon be scrounging for the Benjamins, too.

As hustlers and homeless people alike beg for some dough, you would be wise to keep an eye on your wallet. When you're smooshed in the subway car, you may notice a few advertisements on its wall. One of them being, "Stay alert at all times." They weren't kidding. Keep your hand on your totebag or purse. For instance, if you were wearing a backpack on the street, on the train you might as well wear it in front of you. Granted, it's not like you're being accosted like you would feel among gypsies in Rome or Barcelona, but being distracted by beggars and buskers or being squashed into a small area only means you should be more aware of your purse.

Now, riding the subway as a straphanger could be quite entertaining if you choose to see the humor in it. There's the dude with the funky hair and the sign that reads "Earth Angel." Then there are the guys who rap and dance amidst the car when there are fewer passengers and there's room for back-flips and break dancing. (So not kidding!) Then there are the mariachi guys who play fun music with maracas. Olé!

Cabbing It

Back to the curfew and cabs: If you decide the subway is not in your cards after a specific hour or perhaps even in the morning at an obscenely early hour, it's time to hail a taxi. Another reason, of course, is when you have no clue where you're going. Let's face it: You can become a true-blooded Manhattanite and still need to MapQuest directions to the happening after-party during Fashion Week. When you get lost and time is of the essence (for instance, yours truly always has a hard time navigating Alphabet City!), it's worth the few bucks. Or, you can split it.

For instance, if you're going downtown to the West Village and you're not sure exactly where you're going (since that's where the grid stops and funky streets in various directions begin), do what I do. Take a train to Union Square. From there, hop in a cab. It'll be less expensive than taking the taxi from your original destination and you'll save the time and frustration of getting lost and constantly asking people where Gansevoort Street is. Plus, if you're going out for a girls' night out, you'll get to split the fare a few ways. Yet another way to save some coins. This is assuming you'll be going to a fun evening destination!

Fun Stuff on the Cheap

How do you get in the know, so to speak, about fun things to do on the cheap? You read, darling. After all, it's fundamental. Okay, cheesiness aside, it's really how you get your social game on. On most street corners you can find a printed copy of the *Village Voice*. (Did I mention it's free?) Snag that or check it out online. *Time Out New York* is another must-have publication, also online. You'll quickly be in the know on what's happening every week.

Definitely be on the lookout for free events! Perhaps it's an author promoting her book at a Barnes & Noble. You don't have to pay a cover charge and you don't even need to buy the book. Score! Or perhaps there's a free exhibit at Grand Central Station; you may want to check it out during lunchtime. See, there are ways to infuse your jam-packed day with the New York Experience. You don't need to rely on Saturday night. Better yet, you shouldn't. After all, assuming you've been paying attention, you know that Saturday is, repeat after me: B&T night. Good, I knew you could.

So, You Think You're a New Yorker?

Every New Yorker knows how to walk fast, talk fast, and, most of all, pronounce Houston correctly. Sure, it's a main street downtown. But it's not Houston like the city; instead it's pronounced *How-ston*.

(CONTINUED)

Anyway, Nueva York was originally called New Amsterdam. It began in 1624 as a Dutch fur-trading settlement. In 1625 construction began on a citadel and Fort Amsterdam on Manhattan Island, which was later called New Amsterdam. Well, Manhattan was acquired in 1626 from Native Americans in exchange for trade goods worth 60 guilders (ahem, 24 bucks, thank ya very much). In 1664 the Brits conquered the island and renamed it New York after their Duke of York.

As for its nickname, the Big Apple? The term was used first in the 1920s by a sportswriter, John J. Fitz Gerald, who wrote for the *New York Morning Telegraph*. Tourism triumphed; and since the 1970s in particular the term has become synonymous with New York City.

Broadway and Off-Broadway

For Broadway you can try to get student rush tickets, which are usually distributed 30 minutes before the show. Or show up at the show's box office on days the theater will likely be empty (Super Bowl Sunday, anyone?). Or simply go to the TKTS booth in Times Square. You have to purchase tickets a few hours ahead of time the same day of the show, but there are significant savings. Now, as you're juggling your work life, social life, finances, and the like, you may forget that Broadway exists. Sure, as you first arrive you'll be mesmerized by the ability to check out the Great White Way. Please remember it exists when you become immersed into your life. Sometimes on a rainy Sunday afternoon you'll want to stay curled up in bed with a cup of hot cocoa, and that's perfectly fine. But if you choose to stay home or get caught up in your own social swirl, you may soon forget all of the incredible cultural happenings Manhattan has to offer. Live theater is one of 'em.

When out-of-town friends visit, you will definitely remember that Broadway and Off-Broadway shows exist since they'll likely want to see a show. But you won't want to miss the latest Hugh Jackman performance or good ol' fashioned theater. Off-Broadway shows are also entertaining, and guess what? They're often cheaper. A typical Broadway show may cost you upwards of $75 for each ticket. As for Off-Broadway? Let's just say it could be a lot less, and you could actually afford a meal afterwards.

Movies

And how about the silver screen? If you go to an AMC movie theater for the first showing of the day on weekends, you'll pay six bucks, typically half the price of a regular ticket. Granted, you won't always want to catch a flick at 11 in the morning; but hey, how many movies are really worth the full amount, anyway?

Art and Culture

In addition to live theater and movies, there's always art! (You culture vulture, you!) Can't possibly stomach the 20-dollar admission fee at the Met? Never fear. If you go on Friday nights it's pay-as-you-wish. Translation: Give a few bucks instead of the whopping 20 and you're totally cool. Technically many museums are pay-as-you-wish; they just lead you to believe it's a standard fee. But, to me, pay-as-you-wish is just that, a buck? Free perhaps? For instance, there is no place I'd rather be on a Friday night than at the Met. Usually there's live classical music, it's not too touristy-infested, and their rooftop garden from May through October is simply to die for with views of the park. Ahhhhh.

The MOMA is also free on Fridays from 4 p.m. to closing, as are other lesser-known magical museums like the Morgan Museum in Murray Hill. All you need to do is check out their Web sites and voilà! The city's art and its archives are at your fingertips. The Morgan in particular is not tourist infested (um, I mean crowded with tourists), which makes it completely relaxing on a Friday night when you need to chill after a long work week.

Retail Therapy

Whether you're hoofing it on foot or on the good ol' MTA subway, as you're checking out a new art exhibit you just heard about in *Time Out New York* or you're chillaxing uptown at the Museum of Natural

History, chances are you'll need to eat (duh) and you'll want to shop (double duh).

If you've ever been on a diet, you'll graciously enter a cupcakery only to look at—not touch, smell, or taste—the contents. Yeah, I'm talkin' about eye candy bliss! One whiff of the bake shop, one glance at the case, you're good to go. No calories are consumed, no cash was spent, and most importantly, no one was hurt in the process.

Guess what? The same concept applies to retail therapy. Perhaps in college you went a bit overboard in the mall from time to time or got one too many t-shirts in the campus store. Well, in NYC retail temptations are all around, but this is where the eye candy comes in again: You don't need to consume to reap the benefits.

That's right, if you're having a bad day and need to simply stroll through Century 21 downtown, do that: Stroll. Shop with your eyes and not your wallet. During the holidays when you're mesmerized by all of the artistic department store windows (my fave? Barney's, baby! On Madison Ave., all the way), you won't even have to enter the store to be transported to shopper's nirvana.

What About Online Shopping?

Of course the online shopping thing is always in issue. In fact, in Manhattan I rarely shop in stores. Think about it for a sec: Unlike a mall, in this big metropolis nothing is interconnected. What are the odds all of your favorite stores are right within a few blocks of each other? Moreover, once you start making purchases and have one bag on top of another on top of another, whatcha gonna do with all those bags? Cab it home, most likely. And there goes another 15 buckaroos.

The good news about shopping online is avoiding the crowd and the ability to save cash with shipping codes, but it does remove the retail therapy aspect of going into a store and reaping the mental benefits. My advice? If you truly must buy something, go for it in small doses. As in less than 20 bucks small doses. For instance, if you run out of MAC lip gloss, definitely go to Bendel's on Fifth (so much fun there!). Make it fun; make it snappy; but most of all, keep it inexpensive.

Where to Find a Bargain

I always tell my friends that contrary to popular belief, New York City is not the place to shop for a bargain. Maybe that's because I'm a handbag gal and always get my treats on vacay, but back to you: There are two words here I need to engrave in your pretty little head: sample sales. If you check out TopButton.com, you will always—and I repeat *always*—know when the latest Tory Burch shoes go on sale as well as any other designer whose stuff you've had your eyes on.

In addition, Stacy Francis reminds us to think vintage. "Vintage shops and thrift shops have a plethora of amazing clothes waiting to be discovered." Also, spoken like a true financial guru, she tells us to think ahead in order to save big bucks. "Buy next year's winter boots in March when stores are trying to clear out their winter merchandise to make room for spring items. You will often see discounts of 30 percent, 50 percent, and even 75 percent off."

Shoes, Glorious Shoes!

And now we pause for a commercial break for three divine letters. *D.S.W.*, as in the DSW Shoe Warehouse. It's simply divine. The one in Union Square is a megastore and you can get some serious discounts on all types of shoes, whether it's formal, casual, or super casual (as in flip-flops). Steve Maddens and Franco Sartos and Nine Wests, oh my! You can also become a frequent shopper; and once you spend a certain amount, you purty thing, you'll get coupons mailed to your home. There's also a DSW in TriBeCa (FYI, it stands for Triangle Below Canal, hence the funky capitalization of the truncated name), but do not be fooled, my friend. Yes, it's less crowded than its Union Square counterpart, but it's kinda less fun and doesn't have the same selection.

Saving and Budgeting

Alrighty, we are totally switching gears. As in we were heading cross-town (remember, in this town it's *so* not east or west; cross-town all the way, baby!), but oops, now we simply must go uptown to Inwood. Or all the way to Roosevelt Island (have no idea where it is, but you will most definitely need to catch a tram in Midtown East to get there!).

We've talked about spending money wisely. Now here's a thought: Let's *add* to it instead!

Make Extra Cash

Sure, the technical term is moonlighting, but let's just call it positive cash flow. Although you can easily blow your budget in Manhattan among its expensive restaurants, Broadway shows, and ridiculously high cab fares, it's also a place where dreams come true (don't you ever forget it). As such, it's also a place with oodles of opportunities just beckoning you to explore. Side jobs will bring extra cash into that bank account. There are dog walkers, personal assistants, participants in research studies, guest bartending gigs, weekend DJ gigs, babysitting services, and more.

As for how you find these extraneous jobs? Some of them may be listed in the lobby of your building. For instance, pet sitting is huge. Oftentimes you'll get to live at the person's apartment while taking care of their pet. This means a few days or weeks away from your roomie, and it may just be a ripe opportunity to explore another 'hood. You can easily find out about these gigs through your building, through word of mouth at the office, or through a roommate or friend of a friend type thing.

Another way to find out about these random gigs is through craigslist. Stacy Francis also recommends TREND HUNTER (www.trend-hunter.com) as a place to spot trends and make about $200 monthly. Scha-wing! You can also sell old stuff on eBay or create stuff and sell it on Etsy (www.etsy.com). The possibilities are endless!

Create a Budget

Okay, I purposely warmed you up to save up the best part for last: crunching the numbers. You got money coming in, you got money going out, then you put your right arm in and you shake it all about! (Sorry, couldn't resist!) *What exactly does this mean,* you ask in all italics? It is time to create a budget.

Experts recommend tracking your spending for an entire month and then analyzing it to minimize current spending habits. As for that daily caramel macchiato at Starbucks? Time to cut back to one a week. Once you have your budget, of course the goal is not to exceed it; but you'll need to also start saving a nest egg.

Plan, Plan Ahead

Three cheers for the future! Stacy recommends maxing out your contributions to employer-sponsored plans. If you're into gigging it, she recommends opening a solo 401(k), Keogh, or Simplified Employee Pension (or SEP). She adds, "Whether self-employed or an employee, you can contribute up to $5,000 of your income each year to an IRA. The most important thing is to get started early saving for retirement. Save as much as you can. You get the benefits of long-term growth."

Planning is important to secure your future. A Manhattan lifestyle can suck you in and spit you right back out if you're not careful. You can count on always having social plans every night of the week, and perhaps some nights you'll have more than one option. Check that, you will definitely have more than one option on most nights, and sometimes you may gallivant to and fro! Therefore, you will definitely need to plan ahead. Planning should include a monthly budget plan, a savings plan, and an "OMG get me out of my debt" plan! I'm not a financial planner so all I'm saying is you may want to get one or at least in the very beginning, create a realistic budget and try to stick to it, 'k?

Develop Good Habits

We'll need to revisit some nuts and bolts. After all, now that you're not in college, there are some pretty marvy habits you'll want to get into ASAP in the Real World.

+ The first? Pay cash. It'll give you the feeling that you're actually paying for something.

+ As for another hint? Get rid of credit cards! Experts say to cut them all up. As for Vic's advice? I have only one credit card, which I use 24/7 in order to earn valuable frequent-flier miles for every dollar I spend.

+ Another nugget of wisdom is to never spend more than 50 bucks on anything without taking a day to think about it. "This will curb your impulse to purchase things you really do not need," notes Savvy Lady founder Stacy Francis.

✦ Of course, you should also try to save at least 10 percent of your income each month.

That's a Wrap

In Manhattan you can have a pretty fantastic life. And trust me, you don't need to spend a lot to get it. You'll learn to live on less, in less space, and it'll put you to the test to get creative, be resourceful, and realize that the less you spend on the small stuff, the more you can spend on the big stuff! There will be temptations, whether it's going to Vermont for a ski weekend or joining in on a summer share house in the Hamptons. The key is ensuring that you can afford the lifestyle, or knowing that if you can't afford it now, at some point in the future, if you establish healthy spending/saving habits, you, too, can achieve it. Eventually.

Takeout: Resources to Go

Web Sites

BoltBus: www.boltbus.com

CitySearch: www.newyork.citysearch.com

Etsy: www.etsy.com

Metropolitan Transportation Authority: www.mta.info

NYC Restaurant Week: www.nycgo.com

Savvy Ladies: www.savvyladies.org

Shecky's: www.sheckys.com

TopButton.com: www.topbutton.com

TREND HUNTER: www.trendhunter.com

Periodicals

New York Magazine: www.newyorkmag.com

The Village Voice: www.villagevoice.com

Time Out New York: www.timeoutny.com

CONCLUSION: JUST DO IT!

Diva, this pretty much wraps up *Big Career in the Big City: Land a Job and Get a Life in New York*. Please be kind to yourself during the process, be kind to others, have fun, and remember that your fabulous city-girl-life chariot awaits!

If there was a class in college like "Learning the NYC Ropes 101," congrats, you just passed with flying colors! Let's face it, not everyone has the ability to pick up their bags and move, start their life, make friends, fit in, and settle down. Sure, someone will try to knock you down a few pegs, but you'll be able to pull yourself right back up. You have to. You have no choice!

I've had a blast writing this book, interviewing tons of cool people, and taking notes on what'll make your inner Gotham goddess dance to the beat of your own drum. Most importantly, it's been fulfilling preparing it in a fun way so that you're psyched—not anxious or overwhelmed—to catapult yourself into the Real World in a real big NYC way.

If this was a movie (hey, let's keep fingers crossed; it could be someday! Let's think big, ai'ight?), who should play me? How about Catherine Zeta-Jones? Hmmmm… Who should play your role as the newbie turned street-smart sassy girl? Anne Hathaway perhaps?

It's 'bout time we cue up the closing credits and blast the theme song (*New York, New York,* obviously) while recognizing the magnitude of what you've embarked upon. If you can make it here, you're gonna make it anywhere. By now you're feeling downright empowered and ready to land a big job and get a life (and a fabulous one, at that) in the most spectacular city ever, New York.

The End

(Or rather, it's just the beginning. Go for it!)

Index